An Escape from Communism to a Prisoner of Christ

By: John I. Butura

Printed in Great Britain by Biddles Books Limited, King's Lynn.

Time is too long for those who grieve.
Time is too short for those who rejoice.
But for those who love, time is eternal.

John Bovia

Contents

Foreword

ONE DAY, AS I WAS VISITING with my sister in Christ, Dorothy M, she asked me if I wanted to write a book about my life! When she asked me this question, I didn't know how to answer her. She suggested that I should write about my life, starting with the suffering and the darkness of my childhood in Romania. I knew that there were many souls enduring and suffering as I had, though maybe in different forms, but we all struggle at some point in our lives. There are Romanians who were broken, wounded, rejected, unloved and outcast, and those who were pushed aside, ignored or locked away – ones like me. So, I am writing my story to help you appreciate all of our struggles.

God can still lift us up and use us for his purposes, no matter where we are. If only we listen to Him, He will set us free. He has done it for me. Look to Jesus Christ. He will change you and restore your life. After all, the essence of being human is to struggle and suffer and, in this essence, Christ's life charts our own.

Acknowledgements

THIS BOOK COULD NOT have been written without my good sister and wise friends, who helped me and supported me in their prayers.

I want to give special thanks to my sister, Dorothy M, for the encouragement to step out in faith and to give you my testimony, for all her support and prayers, especially for me to have loosened my tongue to tell you my story of redemption!

To my friend, William L – thank you for helping me to put together the story, and editing my writing and language.

To my friend, Emily M – thank you for the advice, I really appreciate it very much.

Communism — The True Villain

AFTER WORLD WARS I AND II, Romania had been razed to the ground by the German army. In 1952, the president of Romania was Gheorghe Gheorghiu-Dej. He remained in office until his death in March 1965. I was only 8 then, but I can still remember that time very well. The country was poor and the people struggled with many burdens. They worked long and hard to meet their expenses. Romanian families are very large: 4 to 10 people. (John was not the only rabbit.) Most lived in state-supplied apartments or in private houses.

There wasn't much technology back then, so everything was done by hand. The big problem then, as now, was the scarcity of good jobs and good housing. It was hard to find rental property. Everything was under construction or being renovated. Romania is very beautiful; it is like a little Garden of Eden. Then, it had about 24 million people, not much more than the state of Georgia. But the Romanian people were ethnically very diverse. Romanian is the official language, which came from the ancient Etruscan tongue of Italy. The Daco and Romano tribes formed the country of Dacia. Later, Dacia became known as Romania. My language is spoken slowly and calmly and without the Italian habit of flopping one's arms. In some areas of the country Hungarian, German, Yugoslavian and Russian are spoken. The people are really friendly and very trusting. They love wine and beer with their meals. The people also like to party and have a good time. I can remember everybody being happy and pleasant. Before communism, I walked in my neighbourhood night and day without fear of harm. The Romanian people were agrarian, peaceful, and good-natured. The only truly cosmopolitan city was Bucharest, the capital.

Romania is divided into 4 big states and 39 regions. Transylvania is in the northwest of the country. The western border is with the former Yugoslavia. To the north is Russia / Ukraine / Belarus and to the east is Moldova. In the south are the Romanian states of Oltenia and Dobrogea, which border Bulgaria. The people of Transylvania are from all over Romania. They are Hungarian, German and Yugoslavian! Most Romanians speak two or three languages. The beautiful Carpathian Mountains enter the country from the north and make an "S"-shaped curve towards the south. They are high, with many huge lakes among the peaks. Oak, beech and coniferous forests cover the mountains. The mountains are rich in zinc, coal, iron, copper, rock salt, gold and other minerals. In central Transylvania there is a high plateau that has everything: farms with cattle, sheep, pigs and chickens, and forests with wild animals. Transylvania holds the riches of the country. Most of the roads in Transylvania are good and hard-surfaced. Transylvania's capital is Cluj-Napoca.

Before communism, the Romanian people worked hard on the land and lived to an old age (70 to 75 years). Everyone got plenty of exercise: you either walked or took public buses or trains. Every family in Transylvania had a farm or a business. Even poor shepherds were well off. Most had 500-1000 sheep and had good grazing land all over the Carpathians. All of the farms had cattle. There was never a shortage of meat or cheese. Everyone was fed in the cities. Before communism, it was a land of plenty: lots of natural and fresh vegetables and fruits. Our own farmers provided us with what we needed. They were free to sell their goods on the open market and everyone prospered. And Transylvania had a lot of arable land, so agriculture was very important. The people in Transylvania back then had the freedom to own businesses, houses and other properties. They were also free to travel anywhere, even out of the country. Food was in abundance. The grocery stores had everything.

Religion in Romania was unregulated and not stigmatized. People made their own choices. The largest churches were the Roman Catholic and the Orthodox. There were other Protestant churches. The Catholic Church was recognized by Rome.

Another beautiful state (now no longer a part of Romania) which was to the east of Transylvania, was Moldova, which bordered the Ukraine. West of Transylvania was the state of Oltenia (or old Romania). To the south is Dobrogea. Moldova had Iasi as its capital. There were several other big cities surrounded by mountains. Moldova didn't have much land of agricultural value, but the people specialized in forestry and viniculture. Hundreds of acres of vineyards were all over the hills and mountains. Most people from Moldova lived in small towns or cities. There was a big difference between Moldova and Transylvania, even in the dialects spoken and culture. Moldova was much poorer than Transylvania. People from Moldova had to work in migrant jobs and leave their families for long periods of time. As a consequence, their families were unstable.

The big rivers, Siret and Prut, provided plenty of water. The Black Sea provided fish. The biggest fish company was found in the city of Tulcea. This city was recognized all over Europe for its fish products and vegetable exports. People grew their own produce and most of the people had their own land. The families in Moldova were between 6 and 15 people per house. Moldovan people lived very simply.

Another beautiful state found in the southern part of Romania is Oltenia. Oltenia is bordered by Bulgaria in the south, Transylvania in the north, Yugoslavia in the west, and Dobrogea on its eastern side. There are lots of rivers crossing Oltenia and many tributaries of the Danube river. The Danube river separates Romania and Bulgaria for a long distance. Then the Danube goes inside Romania from Dobrogea, which is a Romanian state, and then empties into the Black Sea. In Oltenia, Bucharest is the capital of Romania and it is in the centre of Oltenia. All roads and railways pass through Bucharest. The whole state is arable, has very good ground and is the largest contributor to Romanian agriculture. Oltenia supported the whole country with bread and vegetables. Most of the Oltenian people are farmers. Most of Oltenia belonged to the government of Romania. The petroleum industry is centred in the city of Ploiesti. The Dacia Company made small cars in the city of Pitesti. The car company was a large employer. The people there spoke a different dialect from official Romanian.

Craiova was another great industrial centre with heavy industries: fuel, machinery, and transportation equipment. Farm equipment for export to all of Eastern Europe was made in Craiova.

Another small state was Dobrogea, with its capital at Constanta. Dobrogea was bordered on the south by Bulgaria and the Black Sea, on its west side by Oltenia and on the north by Moldova and a good part of Russia. Here, people primarily fished and wove beautiful rugs. The big cities were on the Black Sea. Constantan and Mamaia had the most beautiful beaches in Eastern Europe: tourists flocked there in the summertime, and many Romanians spent their vacation on the Black Sea beaches and cities. The Dobrogea port on the Black Sea received goods from all over the world. Constantan had a large shipyard, where freighters were built and repaired. It was a tradition in Romania for the people to spend their vacation here – not counting the cost.

Under President Gheorghe Gheorghiu-Dej, Romania began to provide social services such as medical care and pension plans. All these benefits were free and everything was covered. I can remember that all the people loved the president. When Dej became president, he accepted the communist system, under the heel of Russia. That period of communism was not so bad, because people helped each other. There was unity between them. Then, in that time, communism was more by choice and not by force. Early on, the Communist Party was in very good communication with the people. The government cooperated with the people. No pressure or restriction was placed on anyone, and the government usually considered the public mood and desires. The Communist Party was for one purpose: people all over the country were to help each other, especially the poor. And the people from Romania lived in perfect peace, good harmony and joy, so everybody was happy with what they had.

In March 1965, the entire country was shocked when the president died. The whole country stopped to mourn for him. For the whole week there was nothing but the funeral of the president, Gheorghe Gheorghiu-Dej. There was much sorrow because the president was gone and people didn't see peace without him. This president could walk by himself: he had no escort or security after him. He was popular, friendly, and loved by the country and all of the people. The radio station, TV and newspapers continually mentioned the good things he had done. Most offices shut down for that week. The trains ran free of charge to bring the mourners to Bucharest. The president was a man of integrity and was well-respected in government. He had been accessible to the common citizen. He was a very simple man – not looking for riches!

Gheorghiu was succeeded as president by Nicolae Ceausescu, with his wife, Elena Ceausescu. He was born on 26 January, 1918 in Scornicesti, a very small town of no particular importance. Most of the people there were farmers. The town was a suburb of Bucharest. In 1939, he married Elena Petrescu. She was born in Oltenia. In August 1944, he had been released from prison and became secretary of the Union of Communist Youth. While in prison, he had met Gheorghe Gheorghiu-Dej (before he was president) and they became good friends. In 1950, Ceausescu was appointed the nation's minister of agriculture. By 1954, he was a Major General in the Army. He became second in command to Gheorghe Gheorghiu-Dej. Then, in 1965, Nicolae Ceausescu became head of state as well.

In 1974, Ceausescu was re-elected as president for life. When he became president, everything went smoothly for several years. But the peace began to deteriorate. When Ceausescu finally came to full power, everything changed for the worse. In a very short time, the prominence of the security forces increased. At that time, nobody fully understood why. When he had become president, Ceausescu made many promises, but what we got was an iron fist. Within two years, the shadow of darkness had fallen over Romania. The whole country was disoriented. The security services became the worst lawbreakers. We were terrorized. Fear rested on our country.

The disaster started in 1970. New laws took our freedom away. The new political divide was between the poor people and the Communist Party members. Ceausescu's first step was to export our food for hard currency, as Stalin had done in Russia during World War II. In the process he starved the poor people, also like Stalin. A country which had been a cornucopia came to the verge of starvation within several years. But nothing could be done: it was an internal problem within Romania. The president, Ceausescu, had all the power and a well-fed Communist Party backing him up. Almost all pork, beef and chicken was for export, as was the corn, wheat and vegetables. Everything was for sale abroad. President Ceausescu said that we should help other countries because they had no food, but Romania was brought down to starvation. Women and children had to stay in line from 2 a.m. till 7 a.m. for two litres of milk, or fat and bones. Gone were the sugar, cooking oil, meat, bread, eggs, cheese, wheat flour and corn, and there was no coffee, sweets, etc. Then the government seized all private land and factories. Thousands of farmers lost their farms.

All these things were taken by force. No money was given. Many people were forced to live on the streets. The government provided only small, cheap apartments, and then only to the party members. To join the party you had to agree to blindly obey Ceausescu's government and to submit to draconian laws. And, of course, everyone who joined the Communist Party got what they needed: good jobs, food and housing were made available. But those who resisted were either slowly worked, or starved to death or into complete submission. President Ceausescu broke the will of an entire country. The people lost their identity and character. The president turned these people into dirty, feral animals. Ceausescu was in control of the Communist Party, and the party was against the common man. Everything belonged to the state. Even the tourism stopped, Because tourists found that food prices were too high. But the real disaster was for the poor people.

Everyone suspected that the source of the destructive greed of the new regime was actually the product of Elena, Ceausescu's wife. Other people thought it was his whole family. But President Ceausescu was ultimately responsible. His rule was the worst disaster ever in Romania. The economic and social fabric of the entire people was shredded: from the Garden of Eden to a vicious, heartless jungle in less than ten years: the poorest country in Europe. The hospitals were empty, because there was no medical assistance, medicine, or other supplies. Doctors, engineers and all the professional classes fled. There was no one to plan or rebuild, only greedy party members and starving ordinary people. Power and water were rationed – hot water was provided for two hours once a week for apartments. The whole government of Romania was controlled by Ceausescu and his wife, Elena. The truth is that Elena was in control. President Ceausescu also appointed Elena and many family members to high posts in the government! Ceausescu was manipulated and seduced by his wife and relatives. She chose to ruin the country and he let it happen. She was another Jezebel who continually did evil. She influenced authorities by giving them the power to do whatever they wanted. Her first priority was her relatives. She had nothing for the common people of Romania. She, like Nicolae Ceausescu, was full of empty promises. A hard, cruel woman with no compassion! She was an uneducated woman – country-come-to-town. Her speech was nonsense and very aggressive. Whenever they spoke in public, they promised to bring back the old, prosperous Romania. More lies! When they visited other countries, thousands of people went to Bucharest-Otopeni airport to see them off. When they returned, it was the same way; they were showered with flowers. The Romanian national anthem became a funeral dirge. The people's "welcome back" was as hollow as the Ceausescus' promises. A very long, red carpet, which they both walked on, was the blood of the Romanian people. Their rule was nothing but smoke and mirrors. Ceausescu's name was written everywhere. Banners, newspapers, pictures, books, TV and radio stations were all about him. Only the Communist Party had any political voice in Romania, and Ceausescu made all of its speeches. The people who welcomed him at his public appearances were paid to do so. That was their job. They were all Communist Party members who supported him. When Ceausescu visited cities inside the country, plans were made months in advance. Everything was cleaned and painted; flowers everywhere. Everything was immediately fixed, no matter what the cost. When he came, everything stopped for his visit. Hundreds of security agents were everywhere, like ants. He was surrounded for protection. But the bulk of the security was for Elena when she was with him. The Ceausescus lived in Bucharest, in a secret underground bunker. Security details watched them continuously.

Previously, the churches had been free and people could choose their religion but, in 1972, the churches had to start cooperating with the state. They were treated badly and persecution became the daily norm. Lots of Christians lost their jobs. They were ridiculed and given poor jobs to show what their religion was worth. Many gave up church so they could get better jobs and eat. Christianity was not considered or respected any more. The churches weren't allowed in the cities, either. They were exiled to the suburbs. If something bad happened in the city, the Christians were blamed for it. The government disavowed God, and the name of Jesus Christ was never mentioned in public discourse. There was an inverse relation between Christianity and the Romanian government – the more you believed, the worse you were treated. Christians could not work or hold positions within the Communist Party. Nicolae Ceausescu and his wife never mentioned the church, not once. So, the church was only for the poor people and not for the Communist Party.

Living in Romania became worse, day by day. Chaos reigned. Lots of people from Valea Jiului wanted to leave the country, but the security forces of the state wouldn't approve their exit papers. Some people fled illegally – rats getting off a sinking ship. Lots of people escaped, but many more of them just disappeared. Sad stories at the border! Families were torn apart. The security apparatus made the entire country miserable. We became a violent and riven nation.

In the Beginning

I WAS BORN IN MARCH 1957, in Romania (a communist country). From the age of 6 I remember things which will always remain with me, and most of them are bad. But they are part of my life and journey, and can't be ignored.

To the extent that I was raised at all, I was raised by a single mother. I never knew my father and my mother never told me about him, though I asked often. Many times, I wanted someone to call "father", but my mother didn't understand. My mother was 16 when I was born, so I am sure her memories weren't very pleasant either. My first years weren't all that bad. We had an extended family (my mother's parents mostly, plus her brothers and sisters.) Everyone took care of "the baby". But, eventually, my mother had a hard time finding a good job and her own apartment. When I was 6, the Romanian economy was good: food was plentiful and everyone was happy. Then, the president of Romania was Gheorghe Gheorghiu-Dej. He was a very patriotic man and loved the country, and times were good.

I remember that my mother and I lived with an old boyfriend of hers because she didn't have the money for her own place. Her trade was repairing miners' lamps. Romania had lots of mines and, therefore, lots of miners. She worked 10 - 12 hours every day just to take care of us. We lived in Lupeni, but I didn't live there long. My mother, out of economic necessity, sent me to the country to live on my grandparents' farm. I was very uncomfortable with them, because they really didn't want me. They never held me, talked to me, or provided me with the affection any child needs. I was a stranger in their home. My goal became to go back to live with my mother. Every time I ran away, my grandmother beat me and bruised me all over my body. I started to despise my grandparents and I had nothing in my heart for them. The beatings made me worse. All my grandmother cared about was me working hard on her farm. I came to hate them all – grandfather, uncles, and everybody around me. I saw that nothing would satisfy my grandmother. Finally, my mother came and got me because my grandmother couldn't contain me any longer. I tried to explain my anger to my mother, but she had her own problems and was unable to understand a child's mind. I was rejected by every one of my relatives.

It was a shining day when my mother came to take me with her to the city. But soon I felt lonely again. After a while, my mother put me in a school in first grade. I didn't like school, because I could not abide being around strangers. I had no friends. Most of the time I was isolated (self-imposed) from the other children! Almost daily, I cut class and headed off on my own – to the street life. I walked the streets with no sense of purpose, just looking for trouble. I cut school a lot. When students in my same class came to my door with notes from the teacher, I would take the notes and never give them to my mother. Sometimes I went to school and my teacher would ask me if my mother was home. I would say, "No, she's working". My mother was always tired, working lots of overtime. She didn't have time to control me or help me. When she asked me how school went, I assured her all was fine. Needless to say, I didn't pass the first grade. Well, my mother explained to me that she was looking for another place to stay, but that I would have to go back to my grandmother's farm. It was true; my mother couldn't afford to take care of me. I had few clothes, and what I did have were hand-me-downs from our neighbours. My shoes had holes. In cold weather, I stuffed them with cardboard. I was a little hobo. Romanian winters are hard, cold and white. I tried to go outside and play and sled with the other children, but I didn't have the clothes or shoes to stay long. I tried many times to stay outside to play with the neighbourhood children, but I couldn't handle the cold. So, again, my mother decided to send me back to my grandmother's and to spend the vacation from school on the farm. I hated it, because I had to work hard and had no time for any childhood distractions. When I was back on the farm, my mother talked with my teacher and discovered how poorly I had done at school, so she decided to let me stay on the farm until I finished elementary school, then bring me back to the city.

My mother lived 5 hours away from the farm. We travelled there by train. My mother lived in Lupeni but the farm was in Geomal, near the city of Teius. I had to restart the first grade in Geomal. I didn't know anybody there. The teacher was nice to me, but I didn't pay too much attention in class. I went to school in the morning and, in the afternoon, I worked on the farm. I slept in the barn and ate separately from the family. I knew I had to stay there for 4 years. I kept complaining to my mother, but there was nothing she could do. Then I stopped telling her how I was treated. The next time my mother came to see me I just stayed outside, keeping myself busy to avoid talking to her. I had no love for her any more. I had a pair of shoes every year. So, in summertime, I walked barefoot. I put my shoes on just when I went to school. I had two pair of pants, a couple of shirts, one jacket, and not much more. I had just the bare necessities. In Romania the summertime did not get much above 70 to 75°F. But in the wintertime, it was very cold – down to 25 degrees below zero. Winters were heavy with snow and ice, especially November through to March.

Things got worse at my grandmother's house. My two uncles despised me. The older one was a shepherd. The younger one stayed at home with me. But there was a big difference between him and me. He was a mama and daddy's boy, whereas I belonged to nobody. I had to go into the basement of the house and steal bread to quell my hunger, or steal some pork sausages or fat back. The house was small. It had two rooms: one was for daytime and the other for sleeping, but not for me. I had my place in the barn with the cows, pigs and chickens. My mother's family were very poor and worked hard just to survive. They had two cows, which pulled the wagon and ploughed. They had their own land, which was planted with corn, wheat and barley, and a small garden for the vegetables. Everything was made by hand. They had apples, prunes, pears and peach trees.

I never stopped working. Summer or winter, there was always something to do. In wintertime we had to go to the forest to cut trees with an axe. We carried the wood on our shoulders to the wagon, which was pulled by the cows. It was very hard work, especially when it was cold and the rubber boots had holes in the bottom. I didn't have much fun, working all the time. I hated it when I had to go to bring water from the well, or when I had to use the bathroom. There was a special place in the back of the barn for me.

Both of my uncles went to the movies on Saturday nights, but I had to stay home. I wasn't allowed to go. I didn't have the proper clothes. I was an embarrassment to them. I ate lots of fruit and vegetables, fresh, without salt or black pepper, but I was happy to have them. When I wanted to eat sweets I would wait for our neighbours to leave home. Then I would sneak into their barn and steal a few of their fresh eggs. Then I would go to the grocery store and swap the eggs for sweets. I knew 3 big eggs would get me 16 sweets. I would run home with my little bag of sweets. I ate them quickly, so no one would see me and ask me how I got them. The neighbours knew I was filching eggs, but they couldn't catch me and probably didn't want to. But they started turning their big dogs loose when they left for their farm fields. They thought the dogs would bark and bite and I would stop. But the dogs were my friends. Nature was my enjoyment and recreation. The more I grew, the harder I had to work.

In 1965, President Gheorghe Gheorghiu-Dej died. He was the head of the Communist Party from 1952 until 1965. Two years later, the president of Romania became Nicolai Ceausescu. In 1974, he became president for life. I didn't understand at that time the harshness of life and the bad laws. Then the strong weight of communism rested heavily on my country. The whole country had changed by 1968. I remember, I was still in the fourth grade and I didn't know how to multiply or add. But I got specialist training in agriculture. I learned how to plant corn and tend a vineyard. I enjoyed agriculture. The school wasn't big – the whole building was just two big rooms with about 25 students in each one. It had another small room for the two teachers' private use. The town of Geomal was small, with dirt roads, one school and one small store with food and farming supplies. There was one Catholic church. It had two hundred families. Everybody knew everyone; anonymity was impossible.

In 1968, the older uncle (the shepherd) left the town and went to live with my aunt. Her name was Jenica. His name was Peter. She had left the farm when I arrived. Later, she stayed with my mother in the city of Lupeni. Two years later, Jenica moved to a big city called Timisoara (in the region of Banat), where she got married. In that time her brother (my uncle) Peter was looking for a better life, so he gave up shepherding and went to Timisoara with his sister to try to find a job. After about 6 months, he accidentally drowned in the Timis river. He was 17 when it happened. He had gone to the river for fun with other friends, but Peter didn't know how to swim. Everyone was broken-hearted. I didn't like him because he was the one who put all the restrictions on me, so I felt nothing for him. The situation didn't change much at the farm. I had to work more.

There was no high school in Geomal, just the elementary school. I had to go to another town for the fifth through to eighth grade. That cost my grandmother money, so she wouldn't agree for that to continue and, therefore, when school started, my mother came and got me and took me back to her apartment. By her working so many years, the state gave her an apartment with one bedroom and a living room with a kitchen. The bathroom was shared. A very cheap place to live! I was back in Lupeni with no friends. But this time it was 1969, and all was different: my mother had a boyfriend. He was about 270 pounds, 6 feet tall and about 30 years old – Luca. Luca had been a shepherd before coming to Lupeni. He had a brother who was a coal miner with electrical training. Luca now also had a job as a coal-miner, and that is how he met my mother – she repaired their lights. He loved to drink, but drinking made him violent. I had to submit to his authority, no matter what. That was the condition my mother imposed on me when they picked me up. He told me to call him by his name, Luca, and, at first, he was good to me. But it didn't last too long. He didn't care about my mother or me. He paid no attention to me. In fact, he threatened many times to take me back to the farm. Our relationship became unpleasant and then it just got worse. There was no love in Luca for my mother or me. Everything that went wrong was blamed on me.

I was extremely careful in that apartment, because everything I touched caused trouble for me or my mother. We had to listen to the music he chose. We had to listen when he talked. It was better to keep our mouths shut just to avoid arguments or ridicule. I truly was confused, because I didn't know when I could speak. I had traded pressure from grandmother for pressure from Luca. It was too much for me. I felt so crazy. One day Luca came home drunk and he started to destroy everything in the apartment. He was out of control. What a spectacle he made. All the neighbours heard him when he came home upset or drunk, or both. But he didn't stop there; he got his hands on my mother and beat her really badly. She was all bruised and battered. He had no

21

compassion. I knew this couldn't last. I didn't like my mother, but I felt bad about it because I was too little to fight Luca. Then he turned around and began beating me for no reason. He bruised me on my back and legs with his leather army belt. There were welts an inch wide and four or five inches long all over me. I didn't understand his anger. But he beat me for 15 to 20 minutes. At other times, he used a three-quarter-inch rubber hose. My skin was cracked and split due to the swelling. Sometimes he struck me on the top of my head with his palm. When he did, I could see nothing; just colours and little stars sparkled and, after that, I would fall semi-conscious. The more I screamed, the worse he hit me. That occurred many times.

Any time my mother or I arrived home, we anticipated an ugly encounter, which could culminate in a beating. The day after a beating, I looked at my body in the big mirror. I couldn't believe the big marks. The second day the pain was worse. Nobody knew what was going on. I couldn't tell anybody. Luca warned me that, if I opened my mouth, the next time he would kill me. I cried because nobody did anything. My head was swollen. I couldn't roll on my pillow as I slept. My hands were battered because I tried to defend myself. But the most terrifying blows from Luca were his kicks. The pain and bruises from his kicks lasted a week, or much longer than the blows with his army belt. Sometimes I couldn't walk well for several days, and I had difficulty seeing through swollen eyes. My skin looked like the blue end of a rainbow. I was ashamed to be seen in public. I was just a young kid. But I was instructed by Luca not to talk to anyone. He never apologized. My mother was in the same situation. But she had to work. When both of them were going to work, he locked me in the apartment. I had to use a bucket for urination and defecation, because I couldn't go to the communal bathroom. When he came home, he let me go outside to play for two hours only. I had to stay in front of the window so that he could see me. And I was to speak with no one. I had no right to talk to our neighbours. I was seen only. When his friends came to our apartment, they asked him what had happened. I couldn't say anything. I just walked away.

Some of his friends asked Luca why he beat me, and he would answer back that he didn't like me. I had to walk out because I was not supposed to hear their business. No matter how bad the weather – cold, hot, rain – I had to walk out, no excuse, and I was permitted to come in only when he called me. Most of the weekends, I had to stay in the apartment and, for that reason, I didn't have any friends. Sometimes, my mother and I had to walk away to our neighbours and hide because of Luca. I would peek out of the window from a neighbour's apartment so I could see if he was drunk when he got home. If he was drunk, we stayed away as long as possible. Payday was an especially fearful time for us. Money bought liquor and liquor brought violence. He would beat both of us, so I started running away from home. I told my mother that, if the police stopped me, I would have to tell them why I ran. I stayed away. I walked around in that city (Lupeni). At night-time I'd go into a basement and sleep near the heating pipes where warm water was provided for the apartments. I stayed away for about three or four days at a time while the situation cleared up at home. I knew what was going on. I told my mother many times to take our clothes (we didn't have many) and leave and not go back. But she was paralysed with fear and would not do it, so we had to suffer abuse any time he came home drunk. Well, the more he beat me, the worse I was. I began staying away for a week at a time. I tried many times to talk to my mother, but the situation grew worse. My mother hoped that, one day, he would stop all the bad things and we could be a happy family. But it never happened.

I went to school in Lupeni. The city had about 40,000 families. It had a police station, lots of grocery stores, companies, two cinemas, and a stadium where we played soccer and, of course, the streets were concrete and asphalt. Lupeni was clean and it had a big market with vegetable stands. I lived close by, so I walked to school. It was big, about 600 children in the morning and another 600 in the afternoon shift. Through the city ran a small river called the Jiul. There were ten cities in our region. It was called Valea Jiului. The river came from the Carpathian Mountains. It was crystal-clear water but, when it passed through the city of Lupeni, the water became black because coal-mining tailings washed through it. I went many times to the riverbank, especially when I ran away from home. It had fish, frogs and snakes, too. It wasn't deep, about two to three feet in some places, but the river was wide.

I was going to school at 1 p.m. until 6 p.m. I had different teachers every hour for each class. The teachers were cruel. I got beaten many times. For that reason, I despised school; I didn't want to go there. I had no attraction for that school, or the teachers. I went for three years to the fifth grade. I didn't pass, because I was absent over half the time.

Finally, I hit the streets and made a lot of friends who could help me. I started to steal, lie, cheat and etc. I trusted no one. I started fighting with anyone I did not like. I became dangerous, even to my friends. I hated being in that situation, but I had to do something for a living. I stole so much that my friends stopped inviting me to their homes or apartments. And I had bad habits. I was always in the streets. But I did have one good friend from school. We started the fifth grade together, but I stayed behind and he went to the next grade up. His name was Bulgaru. We were together all the time. All our neighbours knew us very well. Bulgaru was the same age as me and had the same thoughts and problems. His father was a miner, who worked long hours. His mother stayed home. She cooked, cleaned, and took care of the children. Bulgaru had another brother, Gheorghe, and a sister, Linda. His whole family disliked me, especially when they found out who I was. Bulgaru was forbidden to see me by both his parents, but he defied them. He provided me with food when I ran away from home. We became like brothers. We travelled a lot together, especially in the mountains.

He was a good fisherman. He caught fish with his hands because the River Jiul was small. After that, he split the fish with me and I ate, too. They were very good. We fished above where the water turned black from the coalmines. When his neighbours saw our friendship grow, they were against us. They ran to my friend's parents and told them all the negative things about me. Some of the things were true, but some of them were not. I didn't often go to his apartment, because I knew his mother didn't like me. Bulgaru's family lived in an apartment with two bedrooms, a small kitchen, a bathroom, a small closet and a balcony. They lived on the third floor, all five of them. I liked the location of my friend's home, because another small river ran beside it. He came to my apartment a lot, because my mum and Luca were always at work. When we went to each other's homes, we ate and then left.

Bulgaru and I decided to beat Luca up so that maybe he would stop beating me or, even better, leave. We talked with other street friends and, sure enough, it happened about a week later. One night, Luca came home with blood all over his face and clothes. I was home when he arrived. I wanted to tell Luca that if he touched me again it would be worse for him. But I kept quiet. He never knew why or who, but I sure felt better. In 1970, we moved to another apartment. This one was a luxury for me, because I had my own room. The apartment had three bedrooms, two closets, a kitchen, two balconies and a bathroom. I was so happy to have a bathroom where I didn't have to walk outside the house, like at my grandmother's farm. It was where I had my first "tub" bath. I was thirteen. The kitchen had no refrigerator or stove. My mother worked hard to fill up the apartment with furniture. Luca only worried about his booze. When we moved to the new apartment the abuse slowed down, but peace didn't last long.

About a month later, the neighbours found out who he truly was. I started running away from home again, because he kept drinking and I thought he would lose control and hurt me. I was tired of his abuse. The neighbours were concerned about my mother and me. When my mother got beaten, the neighbours began chastising him for it publicly. My response, as usual, was to run. The neighbours took me in and fed me very well, and then I would go somewhere to sleep. These were the best neighbours I ever had in my life. The children loved me, too. The neighbours offered my mother and me lots of help and support. They were on our side. Luca sometimes cursed the neighbours, and I told them about it. Lots of neighbours (men and women) turned against Luca, telling him to leave and to go back to his sheep. He was frightened by their criticism. He told my mother to send me back to the farm, but my mother did not listen to him. I never had peace with him the entire time we lived together. Luca had never been married before and he never had children. For some reason his relatives didn't like my mother or me. I heard many times his brother's wife, Ghita, telling Luca to leave my mother because he could get better than my mother, and without children. I told him that I agreed with his family and he should leave. He told me to shut my mouth. My friend, Bulgaru, didn't like Luca either. But Bulgaru loved my mother. The apartment was beautiful and we had good neighbours, too; I loved it. The location was just perfect, because the best stores and groceries were within short walking distances. Cinemas, news-stand, tobacconists, banks and appliance shops were all close. Across the street was a big restaurant called *Cina*. That was the place where Luca usually got drunk. All these places were around my block.

The neighbour's children played soccer. I enjoyed it, and sometimes they came by just to visit me. But it was too late for corrections. They tried to stop me from fighting, but it was too late. I acted like I knew everything.

In 1970, the economy of Romania went sour. I, of course, didn't understand. But the food slowly disappeared from the shops. The meat counters were empty, just bones, and pigs' feet for sale! Butter, cheese (my favourite), sugar, flour (corn and wheat), eggs, cooking oil, salami and coffee all became very scarce. My mother didn't have any explanation, either. The communists choked the economy and everyone suffered. First from the food shortage, then everything else, including jobs. There were hard times in my country. What I did see and understand was an increase in state security activity. Policemen patrolled day and night, everywhere. I remember my mother would send me at 4 o'clock in the morning to the meat store, or for milk, to wait in line until opening time. We all wondered what President Ceausescu was doing with the country. Everybody quietly hated communism. Cooking oil, flower (corn and wheat), sugar, bread and milk were available if you had ration coupons. Without ration coupons, no food! The situation got really bad. The policemen did whatever they wanted. They put lots of fear into the people in the city of Lupeni. Then I saw it wasn't just Lupeni. The whole country was under the pressure of communism! There was no one to make sense of it all. I could no longer walk alone at night.

At the age of 13, I began to think about fleeing Romania. Bulgaru and I talked about it. He didn't agree with me because he feared the consequences, but I kept up the idea. I shared my dreams with him about Australia. He would listen to me, but he didn't want to get involved. He was afraid of the authorities and he was a follower. I refused to be a follower because I saw my rights disappearing. I started to develop my dream. There was something inside of me that kept saying, "You don't belong to this country any more." I tried to explain my thoughts and dreams, but nobody was willing to listen. Even my mother thought I was crazy, and maybe I was, but only for telling her. She was afraid for me. Then I stopped sharing my thoughts with anyone; but I kept them in my heart.

The big company in the region of Valea Jiului was a coalmine. The pay there was highly desirable, but the work was dirty, hard and dangerous.

I didn't want any part of it. I was no longer interested in school but I pretended to go, and then cut class and went somewhere else. My friend, Bulgaru, continued school and went on, but I didn't.

In 1971, things worsened in my country. I contacted some of my street friends and we decided to leave the city. When the plan failed, I went to live in the Carpathian Mountains. I met some mountain people and I offered to tend their cows. They agreed, and started paying me a little bit of money. I had about 30 cows to watch and I enjoyed it because of the freedom. I could see, from my perch in the Carpathians, the whole region of Valea Jiului (that means "ten cities and the river called Jiul"). My employers brought me food daily and, in the evening, someone cooked me a hot meal. I started smoking and, of course, the men I worked for provided tobacco for me.

Sometimes it rained very hard, but it was such a wonderful thing to live there. I never had such fresh air in my life. Lots of fruits – plums, apples, pears, blackberries (they were my favourite) and wild strawberries – grew all over the place. Fresh mushrooms were my favourite meal, cooked on top of firewood. Oh, that smell, I can never forget it. Fresh milk and cheese every day, and I didn't have to get up early in the morning to wait in line. Potatoes, onions, cabbage (one of my favourites) with pork sausages (home-made) or smoked fat back, it was a luxury for me. I didn't eat like that at home, because my mother couldn't afford it. In the cities it was getting worse and worse. Now I understood my mother and I started to love her again, because I realized she had tried her best. I helped her financially and, sometimes, I put aside a chunk of cheese (2-3kg) or bag of potatoes (5kg) and took it to her. I still could not be around Luca, and I never was. I was very angry with him because he beat me many times for no reason and, especially, because he beat my mother.

The cows belonged to twelve families and, every day, the owners came by to see me in the mountains. They brought enough food for me and the dogs. They came about 6 p.m. and, when I got back about 8 p.m., they left for home. The next day, somebody new came. The fresh water of the mountains, I can never forget it. But it didn't last long because summer was almost over. After three months, I went back to my mother and hit the streets. Luca and I still couldn't get along, because I refused to tolerate his abusive conduct. In 1971, I got my identification papers and I was very happy about it. The identification papers are called "Bulletin de Identitate" – it's like a driver's licence.

I was 14 and it was autumn, one of my favourite times. It was a great time to steal fruit from backyard trees. We would find trees loaded with fruit in the yards. Bulgaru and I went around the back to load up with as much as we could carry. Sometimes we were caught by an owner's dogs, so we went to the next location. After we had walked away with the fruit a fair distance, we would sit down and eat it. What was left over, Bulgaru took home. One of the adventures I will never forget was a caper that occurred when we were both very hungry. We frequently pillaged his neighbourhood to find something to eat. One time, we found 3 big jars of pickles on a balcony. Well, Bulgaru sat down and I climbed up on him. Then I reached the balcony with my hands. That was the hard part. Then I pulled myself up with my hands until I reached the top. Well, I took one of the jars (5kg) and handed it to Bulgaru, and then I turned around to jump down. When I looked inside, I saw the residents asleep and the TV (black and white) on. Immediately I jumped down and ran away. After two blocks, at the small river we stopped. We looked around and saw we had escaped. We opened the jar and ate it. The pickles were good, fresh, crunchy and perfectly sour. We were not worried about his neighbours, because we already knew that they were against us.

At that time, 1971, my mother was very sick and her legs were weak. They couldn't hold her up. She had to quit her job. I can still remember my mother sitting most of the time in her bed. Her life became worse every day. Before she got sick, she was a very strong, young and beautiful woman. She was always working hard and she never gave up. It was hard to believe what she was going through. She worked two or three days and the following week she was in bed. Finally, she quit work. The state paid her medical bills. The women from our neighbourhood came and visited her almost every day. There were a few wonderful women who visited. They brought her food. Her friends from work also visited her. She had no support from my grandparents, or anybody else. Luca didn't help, either. I even felt bad for myself because she was all I really had. I was without a father, or brothers, or sisters, and I was so bad that everybody tried to stay away from me. I felt very lonely in this world. My mother never conversed, or shared her thoughts with me. She only gave orders. I was tired of orders from Luca, grandparents, uncles and, now, my mother. And the communist regime pressed harder daily.

I remember that, when that winter came, Bulgaru and I walked around in the streets and we looked for Christmas lights. Not everyone could have Christmas lights (or a Christmas tree), only the rich people. Most people could not afford such luxuries, just as with cars, only for the high-class. The Christmas trees were very rare in my country because of the communist government. And you could not find decorations in the stores. People made artificial Christmas trees. They put the trees up for a few days, then they took them down carefully and put them back in their boxes, the same way they did with Christmas bulbs and lights. My mother never decorated one for me, because she couldn't afford it. I never expected to have a Christmas tree. We were too poor to afford basic food. Not even Bulgaru's parents could afford to buy one. Everything was very expensive. When we went ice-skating, we just went to watch others because we didn't have skates. In the depths of winter, the cold stopped people from walking around. Only the state buses travelled on the roads, which were covered in ice. It was about 40cm thick, and it stayed there until spring.

But this year, before Christmas, Bulgaru and I went into the forest and cut 4 Christmas trees, two for each of us. We carried them all the way back on our shoulders. Moving the trees was difficult because of the snow. We sold the trees and, with our profits, we went to buy shoes. We weren't looking for luxury, but for something warm. My mother couldn't afford new shoes for me. I was in the same grade for the third time. My mother asked me if I would go back to the farm, and I refused. The farm was full of painful memories. I cared for no one on the farm, so I stayed on the streets.

The only person I loved was my Great Aunt Victoria. She was my grandmother's sister. Aunt Victoria lived in the city of Paroseni. It was about 20 minutes by public bus. The city was smaller and was part of Valea Jiului. She had one daughter, Jenica, and was married with two children, Danut, 8 and Carina, 3 years old. Iony was her husband, and he didn't want me around. My Aunt Victoria was the only person I could talk to who understood me. She was the only who was concerned about me. I remember she came to visit my mother and me many times. She often brought eggs, potatoes, apples, pears, onions and more. She lived in her own home and she had a little garden. Sometimes I went to her house to help her with chores. When she found out about my mother and I being beaten, she cried. I stayed lots of times in her house. She took care of me like her own son. She fed me very well. Most of the time I went to her house on the train, because I didn't have any money! The bus was cheap, but I still couldn't afford a ticket.

I was a teenage hobo, so I learned at an early age how to ride trains for free. Sometimes I tried to thumb rides, but usually I hid on the train. The private cars never stopped unless the driver knew me. When I was around my aunt, I felt very comfortable and secure. I knew my aunt loved me, even though she didn't agree with lots of things I did. Any time she asked me something, I told her the truth. Sometimes she gave me a little money for cigarettes. She knew that I smoked, because I didn't hide anything from her. I was open to her and I talked with her about many problems, but she didn't have all the answers to my questions, especially about our communist regime. My Aunt Victoria feared God, and she loved the church. But she never talked with me about religion, and I never questioned her. She worked for about 45 years for the state power company. I told her about leaving Romania, but she never said anything about it. I could see her concern for me; her daughter, Jenica, and her family also knew all my problems and they understood. In some way they blamed my mother, because she put up with Luca. Her children loved me.

Raised by the State

WHEN I WAS 14, I stopped listening to anybody any more. In that time, the teachers at the school could not put up with me. They tried many times to intimidate me, but I was fearless. I listened to what they had to say but, if they tried to touch me, I was ready to fight them right there. The teachers stopped talking to me, and I stopped talking to them. I looked upon them as strangers. In the first and second years, I got beaten many times by them. Now I was ready for revenge, no matter who it was. The principal told the teachers that he would contact the civil police authorities about me and, in a short time, he called the police and told them all the bad things about me. They could not control me any more. They said that, for most of the time, I was absent from school. The police contacted my mother to confirm the situation. They started an investigation about me to see if it was true. Well, I found out later that Luca had a lot of bad things to say against me. He told the police how hard he had been trying to help me, especially with school, but I refused. He said he was very tired because I was rebellious. His alcohol problem was not brought up, or my being his victim. The authorities believed him. I was warned by my neighbours, especially the children, who were my good friends, that a policeman had come to my apartment, but nobody knew why. Three days later, one morning when I wakened, I heard a voice in the kitchen. I didn't pay attention to who it was. The policeman was already waiting to pick me up. He had a big dog (German Shepherd) with him, in case I tried to run. I wanted to die. I knew something was wrong. I got the feeling he was trying to separate me from my mother. The policeman's "lie" was that I had to go to the police station because my identification papers were not complete. I knew this was a trick. I was 15 years old at that time. In a very short time I found myself in a correctional institution in Alexandria, in the region of Teleorman.

I had nothing to say any more. I was seized by the state and institutionalized. I was separated from relatives and friends, and isolated. I couldn't go anywhere. For 3 years and 6 months I had to stay there. The institution was surrounded by gates and fencing that was about 10 feet high. The gates moved automatically. It was electrically-controlled from a building. When I arrived, I had to wait at the gate for my papers to be processed. After I had been waiting for a while, another officer came and took me to segregated housing, where I was for 21 days! I had no knowledge of anything related to the programmes inside the institution. I changed my clothes. They gave me a blue uniform. They showed me my bed. I just looked around, lost. I met a lot of other rebellious boys like me. It was an open dorm with another 20 kids in it. We all had the same colour clothes. It was summertime, and the temperature was higher than in my city, because this region was in the south. For 21 days we couldn't walk anywhere in the institution until we had been enrolled in a class. The children there were between 14 and 18 years old. Finally, after 21 days, I got transferred to the fifth grade. From there, I started school again. My class was a new one that had just been formed. I got to walk all around the institution, and I learned every nook. There were 19 classes and 350 kids. I saw the big board of all the students and classes. There was an elementary school with 5 grades. Then there were different trade classes; mechanic, machinist, painter, upholsterer, cabinet-maker and much more. There was only one entrance to the institution. The gate was automatic. The gate-house was a small building with 3 rooms, two rooms for security and one for visitors! Then a path of 200 metres led to a huge building, which looked like a castle. That was the Commander's office.

When I walked down this path there was a beautiful park on the right and on the left. The park had trees – beautiful willow trees – all around. There were cultivated flowers and no weeds. The benches were painted different combinations of colours; there was one every 10 metres, but in different styles. The grass was perfectly trimmed. I never saw such order before; it was a "paradise" for me. Beautiful hanging plants around the little aisle inside the park laid out in the design of a shrine. It also had two water pumps for the flowers. The office building was connected with the gym and library. On the right side and on the left was our dormitory with the elementary school – with all 5 classes. All dormitories were separated. Each class had its own dorm. We all had individual beds. Metal beds and cotton mattresses! The dormitory was very clean and the floors concrete, waxed and shiny. There was a common bathroom. There was also another building, with only dormitories for the trades.

All the buildings in the institution were red brick and painted red-cream, a beautiful colour. The institution was spotless everywhere. Across a path between the trade dorm and ours was a stadium. It was huge. That's where we played soccer. It had facilities for gymnastics, bowling, jumping rope and volleyball. There was a track inside the big stadium. The infirmary wasn't big, because we were connected to a hospital. But it had medicine and a dentist's office. There were two emergency rooms. Only minors were allowed to stay in there.

If I walked to the left at the back of the institution from the centre path, I could see all the trade shops, laundry, greenhouse and warehouse. If I walked to the right, there was the plateau with the main school, cafeteria and the staff cafeteria. The plateau and the paths through the whole institution were concrete, covered with asphalt. At the edge of both sides of the paths were two-feet-high wood fences painted in blue.

On the plateau we assembled in formation every morning at 7:20 a.m., just like a military formation. The commander of the institution was there with us and, if we had personal problems, we had the opportunity to report them to him. The Commander was a policeman "mayor" and he truly cared for us, especially for elementary schoolchildren. The students were older than us; we were the little ones. Every minor at the institution had to be there – no exception was made. It was one of the rules. We also met at lunch and at suppertime on that plateau, which was run by teachers. On the right side of the plateau was the school, with a cinema connected to it. The cinema had about 500 seats and a big screen. It was like a normal, commercial theatre. The movies were about life under communism. Very rarely, they showed a foreign western. Movies were shown every Sunday afternoon. The theatre was also used for concerts, graduations, meetings, etc. In front of the cinema and school was another plateau, smaller than the first one. This smaller plateau was made of stone, laid down very neatly.

In the school building there was a big room for each class (elementary and trades.) and everyone had his own place. There were two laboratories: Zoology and Chemistry. In the elementary classrooms there were benches and tables and a desk for the teachers, not to mention chalkboards. My classroom had a large map of Romania and several historic pictures and chandeliers, and hardwood floors. In front there were two large windows. Behind the school was an apple orchard. From the classroom windows we could see off-campus to the Bearing Company of Alexandria. This company was the second largest in Europe, and made all kinds of bearings. The trade classes were big, and had lots of materials and pictures of industry. The school had beautiful ceramic (black and white) floors. The Zoology laboratory was filled with all kinds of pictures of animals and plants; the human body, trees, etc; a skeleton of the human body, made from plastic. Different kinds of snakes were in jars. That's where I saw my first palm tree. It intrigued me. It was like nothing I had ever seen before. In Alexandria, I got a palm-tree tattoo put on my left shoulder. The Chemistry lab had all kinds of glassware and different-sized jars. It had everything in it.

Between the cinema building and the big plateau was the cafeteria where all the children ate. The building was very large. In the middle was the cafeteria; on the right side was a large shower. The shower could accommodate 50 kids at a time. We showered once a week. On the left was our kitchen. No children were allowed to work there. The cafeteria was very clean; tables, chairs and floors. The food was very good, but the portions were not large. All meals had meat. It was served 3 times a day, for breakfast, lunch and supper. The food consisted of meat, vegetables, pasta, bread, fruit, dairy products, etc. Most of the vegetables and meat that we had, came from the institution's garden. The meat was our own pork. There were home-made biscuits (my favourite). I ate better there than at my home. In the back of the kitchen was a greenhouse, which was made from glass. There, we raised mushrooms and bell peppers. There was a separate kitchen, where staff and officers and employees ate. They ate the same food we ate. The institution was about one kilometre square and was fenced all around, and policemen watched it. At night, dogs were used on the perimeter. No fights were allowed inside, and were severely punished by the Commander. It was very quiet and peaceful there. Nothing could touch us. Only authorized people could come in. We were protected and, of course, one of the educators (teachers) was always with us. At night all the kids slept. The policemen patrolled and watched over us.When I was transferred to the fifth grade, Ms Deaconu was my governess. She appointed me to be the student commander over the fifth grade (my class). She was in her fifties. We all walked in platoon formation (four columns) permanently. If someone had to go to the medical department, we all walked with them. We all had different jobs, but we were not separated. I was responsible when Ms Deaconu wasn't there with us. She was very nice to us and very concerned for everyone. There was no special treatment or discrimination, no pressure from anyone. We bonded together and we got to know each other very well. I heard so many different personal stories, and it sure helped my learning. Our dorm and class were our cleaning detail and we all worked together. Ms Deaconu

prepared us for the future. She tried her best with all her efforts. In school the teachers changed every hour. We had wonderful teachers; they loved us and were patient with us. Everything was new for me, especially my new friends. I was proud of my new friends and teachers.

The time changed and the cold of October was with us once again, so we changed our clothes for wintertime. The clothes were nice and warm, perfect for winter. Every morning at 6 a.m. we got up and went outside for exercise – about twenty minutes. After that, we came back, made our beds and washed our faces, and then everyone walked to his job. A few of us stayed in the dorm to clean up. At 7 a m., we ate breakfast. After that, all the minors had to be present in formation for personal report. At 7:30 a m., we walked to our classes. Some of us went to school and some went to their shop trade classes. Then we came back at 1 p.m. and for lunch. After that, we had two hours free, most of which we spent with Ms Deaconu. We sat on benches and listened to her talk. She always tried to give us hope and teach us about the communist regime. I was always at her side and I looked at her differently. I always saw her patience and calmness, and I was proud to have her as my teacher. She helped us with our homework. She was always ready to listen. About 7 p.m., we all lined up to eat. After that we walked back to our dorm. We shone our boots for the next day and then we relaxed. At 10 p.m., we were all in bed to sleep until 6 a.m. That was most of the daily programme routine.

The weather got very bad in December and we frequently had 30cm of snow. It was not like living in the Carpathian Mountains. It was a lot of fun to play with my classmates. I did not have to worry about shoes or clothes. This time I was equipped and I could stay out as long as I wanted. During winter vacation, we truly enjoyed ourselves. There was no pressure on us. I spent most of my time in the library, playing chess or watching TV. At other times, I walked on paths with my good friend, Thomas. We talked about all kinds of crazy things. He was from another city and he had come from a dysfunctional family, like me. He had more brothers and sisters, but his family had abandoned him, just like mine did me.

Christmastime came; it was the first one for me there. I had heard lots of rumours about what the Commander did every year. In a short time, I got to see for myself. The Commander made a very big Christmas tree, with beautiful decorations on it. Oh, I felt so much love from him in my heart. I could not comprehend why he was doing these things for us. They gave us little bags with different kinds of presents and sweets. We were so happy. A week later was NEW YEAR. All the institution was off for the evening. They fed us traditional Romanian holiday food. There was chicken soup with carrots and pasta (that is my favourite.) There were cabbage rolls filled with ground pork, rice, salt and black pepper, served with sour cream on top. Two pieces of pork-smoked sausage, fat back sliced with cheese, and half an onion with rye bread. We had vegetable salad and home-made chocolate cake. The Commander was with us, as were the educators and officers. We carried on a lot of conversation with the educators and with the Commander, who was very friendly and popular. He put one TV in the cafeteria and one in the library, because there were so many of us. We ate and talked and the time just flew. At about 11 o'clock, we all walked out onto the plateau and were grouped by class. We had fireworks, and that was the first time I had ever seen any. It lasted for 30 minutes. Then the Commander shot a few rounds from his pistol. After that we walked back into the cafeteria, where we sat and watched TV. At 12 o'clock midnight, President Nicolae Ceausescu gave a special speech; everyone had to listen, but we were not concerned or interested in him any more. We knew all his tricks and lies – he said the same things every year. As a matter of fact, he had brought the country down to starvation. We had everything in there but, outside the fences, it was a disaster. Ms Deaconu didn't tell us everything, but it was much worse.

A year passed, and I adapted to the programme and to the rhythm of the institution. The students and employees became my friends, too. That's how we were. The time went by and it was summer vacation, 1973. We all prepared for a camping trip to the city of Zimnicea, close to the

River Danube. They took us there to pick tomatoes, bell peppers, onions and other vegetables. The educators and security personnel were with us. We sat in small camping-houses and we were happy. We were migrant farm-workers for the month.

The city of Zimnicea was near the border of Bulgaria. It was a purely agricultural area. Everything was owned by the state. The people there wore traditional peasant clothes. They were farmers. The city was also very poor, and the people from the city were decidedly unfriendly. They wouldn't speak to us, especially after seeing a lot of police officers around us. We were accustomed to the police, but we saw their fear of the uniforms. We understood why they didn't communicate with us. I saw no big stores or businesses, and no personal cars. Only tractors, big trucks and buses for transportation! The city had about 20,000 families. The people lived in small houses that belonged to the state. We were located in the suburbs, and there were plenty of peach trees around us. We used water from the well for drinking. Poverty was everywhere. I asked myself how these people could live in these conditions. I had a very bad impression of the place. I didn't know that I, too, would be a victim of the communist regime. That summer was very hot and our "vacation" lasted for 3 weeks, until the rain came. It was in August when we got there. At every meal we had extra fresh vegetables and it was just perfect. A month later, we returned to Alexandria because we had to start school. I truly enjoyed the wonderful experience, as did the entire class. We were all happy. We got to know each other better, but we didn't all have the same thoughts or dreams. I never thought to change my dream about leaving the misery of the communist regime.

My heart was secretly set on fleeing to the west, so I got lots of information from students in my class about the border. They lived in different cities or small towns close to the border. I also heard a lot on the radio and saw movies about other countries. I knew there must be some truth in what I heard and saw. It became my dream to go to Australia, and to find a good, quiet place to live without communism or poverty. After a while, I asked myself what in the world I was doing in Romania anyway. There was nothing there to satisfy me. Everyone had given up on me, especially my mother. In the whole year I received one letter from her. No kind of support, not even a visit. The most painful time for me was Saturday and Sunday, when the parents of the children from my class came to visit. The children returned from the visit full of joy, pictures in hand and a big sack full of food. They tried to tell us how good the visit was.

The institution did not allow smoking inside, but most of us smoked when the parents or other relatives visited; then it was a good opportunity to sneak money or two or three packs of cigarettes into the school. Of course, we shared with each other. But those things upset me in some ways; my mother never visited me the whole time I was there. As a matter fact, she never told me that she loved me, or hugged me and, for that reason, I didn't know what love was. What she did do for me, she did because she was socially obligated, by law. Many, many times I felt very discouraged and without hope. I had nobody to lean on. I was seeking someone to love me, but I didn't find it. My friends from my class were close to me and they truly loved me, but I never knew how to return that love. On the other hand, Ms Deaconu asked me many, many times questions about my family, but I had nothing to say. I didn't want to talk about my mother and Luca – especially Luca coming home and beating my mother and me. I didn't want to discuss the bad things. She knew from my papers that I didn't have a father, or brothers and sisters. She didn't know much about my mother, because I never talked. Ms Deaconu was very nice to me. She had to inform my family (as she did with every child), and reported changes and attitudes as I progressed there. This report was in writing, every three months. She asked me where she could send the envelope and I said that there was no point because my mother didn't care much. She did not insist – I didn't let it bother me too much. The time went by and lots of students returned to school from summer vacation with their families. All I wanted was someone to come and pick me up for the summer – but I was abandoned. So, I had to stay there like many others.

I was ready for the sixth form and I was so happy, not because of the sixth form, but because, in only two more years, I would be released. In a few days, the whole student body would be back once again on the big plateau. The commander of the institution was there with us. But this time we were in a different place: we were now in the sixth form. Ms Deaconu was proud of us. She was our sixth-form teacher for another year. We had a few new students, and they adapted in no time. We changed the classroom and dorms. Finally, I was out of the fifth grade!

Ms Deaconu appointed me for the second year to be the student commander over the sixth-grade class and to be responsible when she wasn't there. When I started the sixth grade, I didn't have time to reflect on all the bad things, because I was busy. When I was in school, time went fast and my mind was more on my future. That autumn, Ms Deaconu took the whole class out to pick grapes from a vineyard. The place was close to the school and we walked there. We ate and ate; the grapes were good. We went there for a few days, in the afternoon. In the morning we were at school. After that she took us to another place to pick apples for another few days. The location was in Alexandria, where we lived: the city wasn't that big. The population was about 30,000 families. All the school employees lived there. After two weeks, we changed our clothes. We had summer clothes and, because the weather turned cold, we changed into winter clothes. This time I had too many clothes. I never had so many clothes when I lived with my mother. The winter was back again. It was windy and very cold, especially at night. All the dormitories had heaters that burned wood, and in our classrooms too. In October, the heavy snows covered everything. In no time at all it was winter vacation. We were waiting on another Christmas and a NEW YEAR and it was the same routine as the last year.

More time went by and summer came. Vacation again! I was so glad another year had passed by. In June 1974, I finished the sixth grade. Oh, what a joy, not because I had passed the sixth grade, but because I had only one more year; I just wanted to be free. At about that time, my mother wrote me to tell me that Luca had moved on – for another woman! My memories rolled back and it was a very sad time. Anyway, it was great news for me, but bad news too. My mother had been destroyed physically and her morale had also been destroyed; she was without hope, and was very sick. I was concerned about her. I knew in my heart that it didn't matter what she had done – she was still my mother. I cried a lot of regretful tears, but there was nothing I could do. I truly regretted rebelling against her, but there was nothing I could do to change it. I began to meditate about how to show her the change in me, due to that institution. I just had a feeling that my mother was in a critical condition and was in a lot of pain. All her life she had worked hard, but she never had time for herself. After Luca came, the situation got worse. We went nowhere. When she took a vacation, we only went to the farm. That wasn't fun, but I had to accept it because I was only a child. I wondered many times why she didn't stay at the farm until I grew up. Why did she have to leave the town? So many questions; no answers. Anyway, to step out at the age of 16 like my mother did, in that situation in a communist country, was a bold move. I wondered how she had made it all of these years – I saw no loving relationship between my mother and grandmother or grandfather. I was never told why. My mother never talked of her mother (my grandmother) loving or caring for her – none of that. Being in the institution made me think a lot about my family and relatives! It was as if none of them cared for each other: there was no love shown between them. I was upset because I could not be with her and do something to help.

I had one more year ahead of me and I had to do other things. That summer we didn't go anywhere. We stayed in the institution. Many of the students went home for the summer vacation. But we were a small class, and we spent most of the time with Ms Deaconu; she knew it was our last year. Soon we would be moving from her class. The whole summer I worked inside the institution. There were lots of gardens and we tended to them. I worked with no pressure. I ate so many carrots that summer, I was a rabbit. They were good, crunchy, sweet and fresh. Sometimes, students walked to the park and lay on the benches or the grass, in the sun. During vacation time we had even more freedom. The Commander didn't care what we did, as long as we stayed out of trouble. Our teachers didn't say much any more. We walked in simple groups, not in military formation, but we still had to stay together. We walked together and talked about the future. All of these things caused me to feel badly about my mother and very bitter to Luca. I was very angry with him, because he did a lot of damage to my mother. Towards him my heart was wounded and could not heal. When it would begin to heal, something would come up and reopen the wound. I had a lot of students in my class with similar family problems. We shared them with each other, because we trusted each other. They understood my situation and I understood theirs. That was my second summer vacation there. The distance between Alexandria and Lupeni was an 8-hour ride on the train. I don't think the distance was the problem. I knew the distance meant nothing, especially when you love someone.

I told my class that next year I would be in the mechanic class. I wanted to know how petrol engines function. I walked around the mechanic shop and looked inside to see what it was all about. I wanted to be a mechanic. When the summer ended, I went to a different class. I had to take a test for the seventh and eighth grades. Then I was transferred into the mechanic class. It was 9 months long. We learned about diesel and petrol engines. Beside the shop there were two garages and two tractors. I was really excited about learning how to drive. I took the trade seriously, because I knew I would need it in the future. The school shop was large and it had 3 engines. They were cut away in different ways for our instruction. The shop was posted with information, pictures, books, parts and different tools on the walls. The mechanic class had already been taught at the school for two years. The classroom was located on the first floor and was much bigger than the elementary classes. Most of our initial learning was memorizing the driver's manual. We had to know all the traffic signs. I had new friends and two new instructors, who helped Mr Gearheart, my primary educator. He was good with us. He was in his late 30s and laughed a lot. I liked him because he smoked. Sometimes, he would drop cigarettes on purpose (because he couldn't hand them to us), pretending he hadn't noticed. We picked them up and immediately smoked quickly before someone saw us. We didn't want Mr Gearheart to get into trouble. He was very friendly and popular with everybody. He lived in the city of Alexandria.

After 6 months I knew all the places around the school's perimeter fence, because our shop was near it. I knew where the best places were to sneak out. All the students smoked so, in my new class, lots of cigarettes were trafficked. Sometimes we got cigarettes when the big tractor went out of the institution towing the big trailer. We helped load and unload materials for the institution. It was searched by an officer when it returned. Some "bait" cigarettes were always found, but that was just a trick. The majority of the cigarettes (maybe 100 or 200 packs) got through, well-hidden. The cigarettes sold inside the institution for 20 lei (the Romanian unit of money), which was very expensive. One hundred packs of cigarettes cost 2,300 lei, and 100 packs of cigarettes from a tobacco shop cost 115 lei. There was a big difference. At that time an employee had about 1,500 lei a month salary. The cigarette money came into the institution through the mail or in packages, hidden with food.

For that reason, I mentioned that most of us smoked, and we also shared with each other.

One day I was to make a cigarette-buying run! I asked what the plan was. I was told I was to take the risk with the money that was already collected from the other students. I got the money for 100 packs of cigarettes. It was in March when it happened. About 7 p.m., I jumped the school fence when darkness fell. I ran to the tobacco shop in no time, never looking back. When I got to the city, I walked slowly so as not to attract attention! I was recognizable as being from the school because of my clothes. I moved quickly, not looking around. I knew all the obstacles I had to pass. After 20 minutes I was in the tobacco shop. I handed the money for 100 packs of cigarettes, and the salesman looked at me, very suspicious, but he didn't want any trouble. He handed me a big box with 100 packs of cigarettes. The transaction was very quick. Then I returned faster than I had come, because I thought the salesman might call the Commander. My eyes looked everywhere. Finally, I got back and through the fence. About 200 metres inside, I dropped the box and, immediately, someone came behind me and picked it up! I walked back to the shop, acting as if nothing had happened. All was calm in the institution and nobody observed what was going on. It took me 35 minutes in all. I set a new record, because it usually took 50 minutes to get it done. That was my first and last cigarette run. I received 30 packs of cigarettes, as my part. I shared with all my friends from my class and from elementary classes, my best friends. Nobody knew anything about it except my instructor, because he had his personal snitch. It was too late to do anything, because all the staff had gone.

As time went by, I was busy all the time. I had learned the trade in the seventh and eighth grades. I had to catch up on everything, and I did my best. In a short time, it was spring vacation again, and the school stopped for two weeks. Most of the time during vacation I worked in the vegetable gardens, which I knew well! That time it was different – I worked for free, and I truly enjoyed it, not like at my grandparents' farm. Finally, the time came for me to be released. I had a mechanic's certificate and a diploma from the eighth grade in my pocket. Oh, what a happy day it was. I had waited for three years and six months for that day. The institution gave me some civilian clothes, because I had no one to send me clothes. They also gave me a little money, and a ticket for the train.

My desire was to go to the store and buy a whole loaf of bread and about two kilograms of salami, and bell peppers with onions. After that, to get on the train and eat, slowly until I got home but, to my surprise, I could not find salami anywhere.

Out of School and into the Void

It was the end of June 1975 when I was released. I went back to live with my mother in Lupeni. When I got into the city it felt different; I didn't know what it was. I arrived at night. My mother had moved from the third-floor apartment to a smaller one because she couldn't afford the big one. It was in the same block but had a different entrance and it was on the bottom floor. She wasn't too happy to see me. Her appearance had changed. After 3 years and 6months, I didn't know what to say. There were no smiles and no joy. Not even "welcome back"; I read her face. She really didn't want me. My mother was the same as always towards me. This time I was thinking differently from before. I realized how hard my mother's life had been and continued to be. She had told me nothing about her parents but I realized later on that, when my mother's father had died in World War II, he had left a great estate in land to my mother. All this land belonged to my mother, because she was the only child. When my grandmother remarried, her new husband didn't like my mother. When she ran away at the age of 15, they took all her land. They stole her inheritance, and then raised a new family on the farm: another two boys and a girl. However, they didn't want my mother there, because she actually owned everything. For that reason, mother sent me to the farm: grandmother was supposed to take care of me. That's why I had been treated so cruelly – I was a constant reminder of what she had done to my mother. I was the lawful heir to the farm, as was Mother. It was my land, not my grandmother's, but my grandparents tried to run us both off. My mother went to Lupeni, found a job, and started working hard just to make ends meet. She was uneducated and had no one in the city except my Aunt Victoria, who lived in the city of Paroseni. Back then it was very hard for a single woman to earn a living. I can still remember when she moved, which she did frequently, and when she worked 16 hours a day because she wanted a better life and to be able to provide for me. At that time, I didn't understand why she didn't have any time for me, but now I can see that my mother really did care. Otherwise she would have simply abandoned me, but she didn't.While she didn't show me love, in my heart I knew she loved me. I was just too rebellious to see it as a child. She suffered a lot because of me. Of course, when she saw me after three and half years, she thought I was the same, but I'd stopped doing a lot of the bad things that I had done in the past, especially stealing and lying. Anyway, my mother was physically destroyed. Her bones had deteriorated, so she wasn't very tall any more. When I saw her for the first time, I couldn't believe it. Her apartment had one bedroom, a living room, a kitchen, a bathroom and two closets. She went to her bedroom and I slept in the living room that night. We didn't talk much that night because it was so late when I arrived. I dreamed for two hours about what would happen next. I had never thought before about the communist regime; yet I realize now that it was the turning point for the whole country. There was a disaster in the supermarkets: all the stores were empty. When I came from the state school, I looked around and realized there were no jobs for me. There wasn't even a decent automotive shop where my mother lived. I began to wonder where I could find a mechanic's job. The problem was that the city was an economic dry hole. There were no shops for small car repairs. I could not work privately, because no one knew me as a mechanic – just as an angry kid. I knew I could work as a miner, but I knew that coal mines were "electric" now, at least below the ground; my training would be wasted. I could work, but my experience wouldn't get me higher pay and it was very hard, dirty, dangerous work and didn't pay well. I hated it, and really wanted no part of it. There were many accidents; explosions in which hundreds of people died without record. I knew I could not be a miner long if I wanted to live, but I had to work in the mines to be able to eat.

I thought about visiting my old friend, Bulgaru, and wanted to see what occupation he had. I went to sleep without making any decision about the next day. When I walked outside the next day, I saw a lot of my neighbours, and they were happy to see me. They were glad that I was back. Of course, there were a lot of questions, but then there were always questions in Romania. My neighbours and neighbourhood had changed a lot in my absence. The kids I used to play with were scattered. Some of them were married. Most of them worked in the coalmines. My friends had changed, too. First, I went to visit my friend, Bulgaru, to see how he was doing. It was a 10-minute walk from my apartment. I met him and we sat down and talked for a long time. After a while, he told me that he had a mechanic's job at the coalmines. He told me his pay was good, and how many clothes and shoes he could buy. I was listening to him and was very impressed. He was happy about his money and his freedom from his parents. I wanted to suggest to him about us leaving the country, but I stopped. I realized he was happy with what he had; he wasn't ready to hear what I wanted to say. I didn't share my thoughts with him, because leaving was impossible for him. I understood how he felt, and he was also terrified of the communist authorities.

My mother was quite ill with cancer. She was in and out of the hospital; at one time she was hospitalized for 6 months. Another time, she was there for a whole year. They experimented on her, but she didn't know it. She had already had the second surgery on her chest before she learned she had cancer. When my mother went to the hospital it was in Bucharest, the capital of my country. It was a teaching hospital, and full of medical students. The travel time between Bucharest and Lupeni was 6 hours by train. When she was in the hospital, I stayed there by myself. I wanted to leave the country, but I couldn't; my mother couldn't be alone. I knew she would break down if I left. I knew she needed my help.

I went to visit my Aunt Victoria in Paroseni. She had worked for 40 years at the state power company, but was now retired. Her daughter, Jenica, moved to a bigger city, called Deva. It was different from Valea Jiului. Aunt Victoria planned to sell her house and buy an apartment in Deva, where her daughter was. It was a 3-hour trip by train. We sat down and talked for a long time, about my mother's situation, job problems, the communist regime and, of course, about my dream of freedom, which would not happen until my mother's death. My uncle had died of old age, and my aunt wanted to sell everything and go to be with her grandchildren, Danut and Carina. We talked about that, too. She insisted that I come to Deva and visit her; she had the same love for me as she did for her own children. When I explained to her how I intended to leave the country, she was worried about me. She warned me many times to be careful at the border because I might be shot, but I reassured her that everything would be all right. She was the only one who understood and agreed with me. I spent a few days at her house and helped her with chores. It was relaxing to be there with her. She was 65, but she could move fast and she was still capable of taking care of a lot of work. She had a rough life and worked hard.

The situation there was much worse than when I left the city 3 years ago. People had nothing to talk about except the pressure from the Communist Party, and the needs of their families. However, nothing was done about the situation, and the communist regime pushed hard to the end to keep the citizens from rebelling. Fear was in every person, because there was no mercy any more. Life was becoming unbearably difficult for everyone. There were drastic changes in Valea Jiului, especially where I lived. I remember I could not get ration coupons because I didn't have a job. I tried to explain that I came from another city far away, but no one cared. Therefore, I could not buy food because I did not have any coupons. I just sat back and wondered how long it would last. Anyway, in a short time I started shoplifting again, stealing anything I could to make money to buy food. I visited the flea market, which had fresh vegetables daily, just so I could have something to eat. I fought all the time. I trusted no one, and no one trusted me. I didn't know which way to go; I was confused. I missed the state school; nothing compared with the teaching I had received in Alexandria. Every time I thought about the life I once lived there, I realized I was in the wrong place now. I started drinking, but it didn't help. Every time I drank, I got sick, or I got a headache. So, I found no relief in alcohol.

A Bucolic Interlude – Buta

AFTER MY MOTHER left for the hospital in Bucharest, I was alone. But I met new friends as I walked the streets. Two of them were Aron and his brother, Ivan. Both of them were married. Ivan had 3 little girls and Aron had no children. Both of them lived in the city of Lupeni, in houses owned by the state. Both of them were in their 40s or older. Aron was the manager of a small tourist camp in the Carpathian Mountains. The name of the camp was Buta, at Mount Retezat, about 2,500 metres high. This tourist camp was open all year. The camp was owned by the state, but was run by Aron and his family. Ivan's wife, Rosalie, and their two little girls lived there permanently (one of the little girls lived with Rosalie's parents). Aron's wife was named Margaretta. She stayed home but, if a big camping group came to Buta, then she would go up Mt Retezat and take care of the cooking. Entire school classes (groups of teenagers from the seventh or eighth grade) came there for vacation with their teachers. In the summer, Aron was busy with all kinds of tourists. When he wasn't busy taking care of Buta, he loved to stay in the bars and drink.

It was December 1975 in the wintertime, and Aron asked me if I would spend time in Buta, helping him. I didn't really know what kind of help he needed. I knew nothing about Buta; I had never been there. But I had heard about it and how beautiful it was there. Besides, I had no real choice, because I was running from the police in Lupeni. My stealing had almost caught up with me. So, we picked a day to meet and go to Buta. The snow in the city was about two feet deep. The weather was beautiful. The biggest problem was the cold. We met at the bus station to go to Buta. Aron had two large backpacks, which we needed to carry with us. They were full of food for the camp.

From Lupeni, Buta was 50km. We had to travel on the bus for 30km and walk the other 20km. There was no mechanized transportation for the last twenty. The road that we walked curved among the mountain rocks. I was informed by Aron that the length of the road was

17km, followed by another 3km on a small path. At three o'clock in the afternoon we left the city of Lupeni. We left the bus at a small town called Cîmpu lui Neag, and we started walking with the bags on our shoulders. The further we walked, the deeper the snow got. The air was very clean; I could breathe there. The road was very difficult to walk because of the snow and ice. After two hours of walking, the snow was one metre deep. Aron had army binoculars, so we stopped for a while to look around. We were on high rocks and we had an unobstructed, panoramic view. A beautiful sight, everywhere I looked down in the valley. Small towns and little roads; we could see everything from up there. At 5 o'clock in the afternoon it got dark. Small lights came on everywhere. It was very quiet, absolutely peaceful. That evening I didn't get the opportunity to explore everything because we started walking so late. Our loads that we had to carry were difficult to manage in the progressively deeper snow. We made three big rest stops. We could see long distances with our lanterns.

After 5 hours we finally got to Buta camp. I was exhausted and I didn't talk to anyone that evening. I fell asleep in no time. I didn't even eat. I woke up in the blue-black cold, a little light showing through a small, frozen window. I began to look around me. I tried to look outside, but I couldn't see anything. The window was frosted over. The cold in the room made me shiver under the blankets. Finally, I got up and walked straight to the kitchen. I was attracted by the warm air that came from the kitchen's wood fire. I looked on top of the stove and found a pitcher of hot tea. I had a cup and went back to bed.

Breakfast had been ready for a long time, because I didn't get up until 10:00 a.m. I was awakened by the smell of the wood fire and the sweet aroma of pine trees. I met Ivan's wife, Rosalie, and his two little girls. We all walked together for a while. They warned me of the dangers of the mountains. That first day was beautiful, sunny and clear. I could see for ever. Aron told me the names of all the mountains and the towns. Our mountain was called Retezat. The mountain peak was 2,500 metres high. From the top of Retezat I saw all of Valea Jiului. The surrounding cities and towns were readily visible. A strong but erratic wind blew continuously and changed direction without warning. The temperature was -15⁰C during the daytime. During the night it was much colder. Frozen trees occasionally fell. They died a clean, peaceful death. The snow was packed 3 to 4 metres deep. Its crust was so hard that we walked on it without snowshoes. I enjoyed the serene beauty of those frozen mountains. There was a small artesian fountain at Buta. Why it didn't freeze, I don't know.

We had to wear very thick clothes, because the weather was so cold. Camp Buta was rough-hewn; literally everything was made by hand. There was no running water or electricity. Cooking was done on a wood stove. In every room there was a small fireplace. The camp had 7 bedrooms, a kitchen, a day room, a bar and a special room just for us. The rooms had small windows (which stayed frozen most of the winter). There were metal beds and wood floors. The camp's exterior was of hand-hewn logs and was beautiful. Inside it was made very cheap and simple. There was no transportation up the mountain, so all the food supplies were carried on our shoulders. Sometimes, Aron would borrow a couple of horses from one of his friends to carry heavy stuff. The state really didn't care too much about the conditions. In the evening, we used petrol lamps. There were no facilities to take showers. The bathrooms were outside in the woods. The capacity of the whole camp was about 50 people. Winter tourists were very rare because of the long distance.

I stayed at Buta for 3 months. I enjoyed the rustic life. Aron fed me and provided cigarettes. In return, I worked like a Trojan. My job was cutting wood for the fire, washing the floors in the rooms, cleaning, carrying water and supplies for the camp and helping in the kitchen when needed. After two weeks, a group of 35 students (eighth-graders) came to Buta from the city of Constanta. The group came with their teachers. There were boys and girls. They came for a winter vacation. I met their teachers and we became friends. They stayed for two weeks. Most of the time I was with the students and we hiked around the camp. We played in the snow. Aron gave us some skis to use. I became very fond of the students. Sometimes the boys helped me with my work. When it was too cold, we stayed in the camp and played cards, dominoes, or other games. After all, I wasn't much older than they were. We talked a lot about communism. They understood very little about the evils of their own government. Their parents supported the regime. But we had a wonderful time together. Every morning the boys begged me for cigarettes. Their teachers warned me not to give them cigarettes, but I gave them some anyway because we became friends. Eventually, we said our goodbyes and they left for home. I remained helping and working hard.

I also met Aron's wife, Margaretta. She came up there just to help with the student groups. After the students left, Aron and Margaretta went back home to Lupeni; most of the time I was up there with Rosalie (Ivan's wife) and her two little girls. Ivan didn't even want Aron there. The tourists were rare, because of the cold. At the beginning of March 1976, I decided to leave the camp and face my life. I can't forget the experience I had up there in Buta's camp. I was so happy to meet new people and to have a little fun. I had never had the opportunity before to relax and feel the true joy of fun.

Into the Mines

ARON DIDN'T WANT ME TO LEAVE the camp, but it was time for me to move on. I knew my mother was still in a Bucharest hospital with cancer, so I really didn't want to go back to her apartment. I wanted to get a job like all of my friends. I decided to go and live with my Aunt Victoria for a while. Her house was a long way from the city and my friends. But Aron offered me a room to stay in at his house. I accepted. At that time, I didn't know their families. When I got to his house, I was thinking of where I could get a good job. Aron told me of a place where I could get a job that paid really well. When I heard about the coalmine "underground" chills came over me. I really didn't want to be a part of that dirty job. But I accepted. We went to the coalmine from Paroseni (where my Aunt Victoria lived) and we applied for work underground.

The process was immediate. I was hired. I paid for rent, cooking, and the washing of my clothes (which were not that many) to Margaretta. I was 19. I got all my equipment from the mine company – work clothes, rubber boots, plastic helmet, an electric lamp and a gas mask in case it was needed. It was very hard work for my age. When I came out of the coalmine and looked in the mirror, I didn't recognize myself. It made me really sad. I thought, "What in the world am I doing here?" In about 6 months, I adapted to the atmosphere underground. The pay wasn't as good as I thought it would be. It was three 8-hour shifts. By living there, I got to meet Margaretta and her parents. They lived 5 minutes away. One evening a few days later, Margaretta invited me to go to her parents' house! I went with her. When we got there, her parents were in the kitchen. We sat down and talked. When they saw me, their eyes fastened on me. They gave me a very warm welcome. I was very impressed. Her father was Glava Ionuts, and Anna was his wife's name. They were wonderful people. Mr Glava was in his 70s and retired from the coalmine. He was about my height, but heavier. He had grey hair, brown eyes and a red face that always had a smile. I knew there was something different about them, but I didn't know what it was. He spoke with such love and compassion to me. I was astonished; I got very quiet and listened to him. I felt such peace, and I wanted to hear more from him. In that time, I had so many problems with myself; I had a short temper and was impatient.We talked about everything except religion. Then Mr Glava asked me if I knew the Lord Jesus Christ. I looked into his eyes and I said, "I don't know what you are talking about." Then Margaretta intervened and stopped the conversation by informing me that her parents were Christians. I had no knowledge of religion, especially about Jesus Christ. I went back to their house many times and I listened, but I didn't know what to believe. I was thinking a lot about the stories from the Bible, which he showed me. I didn't know the truth. We spent a lot of time together talking about the Bible. I found that out he was an evangelist at the Pentecostal Church, and he preached about Jesus Christ. They were very strong Christians and both of them walked in fear of God. I started calling them Grandpa and Grandma, because they made me feel so loved. I got close to them in a short time. I started to read the Bible, but I didn't understand it. I was too proud to ask Grandpa for help. Until then, nobody had ever sat down beside me and explained the Bible like he did. I knew all about the bad things from the streets, but nothing about religion.

It was very hard for me from the beginning to open my heart. I had grown up with a lot of resentment and anger; I didn't trust anyone. I was selfish and volatile and was ready to explode at any time. There was no peace or joy inside of me. I was petrified, worried, depressed and scared, all at the same time. I wasn't much of a talker and I couldn't carry on a conversation. Most of the time I was just thinking about my mum and my dream of leaving Romania but, when I was around Grandpa, it was all different. My attitude and my actions showed love toward him but, really, it wasn't me. I realized that I had learned a lot of things from him. He was a godly man, full of wisdom and experience. He was very trustworthy; a man of integrity, a man who you could depend on. He was full of love for people around him and ready to help anyone. Grandpa never spoke negatively. He and Granny had lived together for over fifty years. At the age of twenty-five, Grandpa had received the Lord Jesus Christ into his heart as his Saviour. Granny was saved earlier than that. Every morning, he got up and prayed until 10:00 o'clock. Even living in poverty, he was happy and full of joy. It was hard for me to understand his ways. I never saw him angry or in a bad mood. Although he had a hearing problem, it never stopped him from smiling. Every time I went to his house, he was ready to listen, with compassion, to what I had to say. By the side of his house he had a little vegetable garden. In the centre he had a little bench where we sat and talked for hours.

That summer was so beautiful; we took advantage of it. He asked me how my job was going and I always assured him everything was fine, but I hated it from the beginning. He had worked and suffered for 45 years as an underground miner. He had always said he was ready to go and be with the Lord. No more pain or suffering to face here on this earth. But I did not understand what he meant. I didn't ask for any explanation, because I wanted to find the answer myself. It was hard for me sometimes to understand what he was saying. He was referring to spiritual things, and my mind tried to understand them in natural terms. Many times, I pretended that I understood, but I really didn't. And he never said anything about me leaving the country, though I'm sure he knew.

Grandpa had three children (two girls and one boy). Their names were Margaretta, Ana and Nelu. Nelu was married to Rodica and lived in the city of Pitesti. Margaretta was Aron's wife, and Ion was Ana's husband. Nelu had one daughter, (Emily) who lived with her mother. Rodica had one son in his 20s who was still living at home. His name was Adrian. Nelu was a construction engineer and Rodica was a nurse at the Dacia Company, which made small cars for export. Both of them were close to 50 years old. Margaretta had one son, Emil, who worked at the Dacia Company as a supervisor. He was about 25. Ana and Ion had 5 children: Nelutu, 16, Nina, 15, Lidia, 11, Margaretta, 5, and Amelia, 4. They lived close by. Ion worked at the same company as I did, at the coalmine in Paroseni, but at a different location. Ion and Ana were about 55 years old. Their family name was Radosav. Nelutu and her sister, Nina, were in a special state school because her father (Ion) could not afford the expenses.

Meeting Nina

I GOT TO KNOW the whole family very well. They respected and showed love toward me. All of them were godly people.

After two months living at Margaretta and Aron's house, I went to visit Grandpa to see how he was doing. It was a cold, dark, rainy evening. When I got to Grandpa's house, I entered and saw he had company. I started to excuse myself and walk back home, but Granny insisted that I come inside and meet their relatives. In the kitchen, which also was a family room, there were 7 members of the family gathered. I met Nelutu's sister, Nina, for the first time. She was about 15 years of age, with long, brown, curly hair, green eyes, and a beautiful, smiling face. We introduced ourselves, and I found out that Nina was the daughter of the Radosav family (Ion and Ana). I gawked at her. She was beautiful. She was very simple, and came from a very poor family like mine. The main difference between us was that she had a father, one brother and 3 sisters; I, on the other hand, was alone. It was the first time in my life I fell in love with someone, but that's what normal teenagers do. She came for just a weekend to visit her relatives. The family had a very strong hierarchical relationship, so everybody came to Grandpa and Grandma's house first. After being together there and sharing their love, each of the smaller family groups went to their own homes. Even Nelu (Grandpa's son) travelled a long distance, 5 or 6 times a year to visit his parents, especially on holidays. I got to talk with Nina for a while. I asked her when she would be back. She said on summer vacation, when school would be over. The next day I went to Grandpa's and grilled him about Nina. Then I started to visit the Radosavs' home more often. We all became very good friends. I got to know the family very well and I trusted them.

Ion Radosav had been married to Ana (Nina's mum) for more than 30 years. They were all very lovely people who cared for others. Ana, Margaretta and Nelu had been raised as Pentecostal. Grandpa had taken them to church since they were young.

In the summer of 1976, Nina and I became close friends. We spent most of our free time together. Even when I worked the second shift, 2-10 p.m., she was waiting for me in front of her gate. I arrived about 11:30 every night, and we stayed there talking for another 3 or 4 hours, until morning. We decided not to have sex until our marriage. It was a decision we made together. We went to the movies and to parties. She was very popular, sincere, and very stable. The family saw all these things, but they knew we were good friends. I had never trusted a young girl like her, but she was different and special to me. She had a perfect love and compassion for me. My trust in her was strong. Finally, my mother came back from the hospital. Of course, we went to her apartment immediately and I introduced Nina to my mother. They felt love for each other. My mother trusted her like her daughter. I explained to Nina about my mother's illness. She understood, and their relationship became very close. We spent all of our time with our families, but mostly we were at her house.

My Aunt Victoria loved Nina, too. We visited each other every weekend. However, Grandpa was still the centre of attention for us, and I truly loved him. He understood pretty much my situation and my background. When I saw our relationship becoming stronger, I shared with Nina my dream about leaving the country. I told her that I was looking forward to a better life without the communist regime. I told her, "There is a better life than this." The country was falling apart under communism. Eventually, there would be nothing left. I told her I really didn't want to work in a coalmine like a rat. The conditions were terrible, especially underground. She understood the situation and we were both in agreement. After 9 months, we were always together except when I was working. When Nina's parents understood our relationship, they tried to separate us. Her parents planned to send Nina away to another city to some relatives. A part of the family became hostile to me, though I didn't know why. Finally, Nina told me one night what was happening. I was shocked speechless. Nina submitted to me, and very little to her parents or relatives.Nina was invited away for Christmas holidays, to her aunt and uncle's (Nelu and Rodica) house. They said it was to spend time together and have a good time. (And to get away from me). It was about 6 hours' travel by train between Lupeni and Pitesti. Nina invited me to go with her. I wasn't welcome, but I didn't know, and neither did

Nina. If we had known, we wouldn't have gone. Margaretta's son, Emil, was very angry when he saw me there. I didn't pay any attention to him. We returned back home after the holidays. We were very disappointed about the Christmas fiasco. I started to change my mind about them. I talked to our grandpa and he said not to pay any attention to them. We decided to marry. I was in my 20s and she was 16. It was February 1977. The weather was very harsh and cold. Both families (her parents and my mother) were opposed to our marriage. They all told us not to marry, because we were too young. We ignored them.Finally, after we got married, we had peace between our families. All the rumours and opposition ceased. It was a perfect marriage. But it was hard to obtain an apartment or a good place to stay, so my father-in-law gave us a separate room in his house, upstairs. He gave us a bed, one table and several pieces of furniture. At last we had a place to put our clothes. It was just perfect. The room was spacious. Also, my mother set aside a room for when we stayed with her. Most of the time, my wife was with my mother, helping her! I was in my second year working in the coalmine underground. I was working all 3 shifts in rotation. Each week I was on a different shift. The night shift was the worst, because I didn't get much rest. Everyone helped us from both sides of our families. I had to keep my job to survive. We were in need most of the time, because of the high cost of necessities and lack of food in the country. We lived very peacefully and loved each other. Soon, all of our family, relatives, neighbours and friends were happy for us.

Labour Unrest – The Personal Tragedy Begins

In July 1977, the weather was beautiful. The days were sunny and unexpectedly hot. At the time, I was working in a coalmine in the city of Paroseni; three shifts, eight hours each. I was scheduled for the second shift, which was from 2 p.m. until 10 p.m. When my shift ended, I had to rest for half an hour. Then I changed my clothes and took a shower. I put on my clothes and walked to the bus station with my co-workers. The mine was about 15 minutes from where I lived in Lupeni, in a new apartment block constructed by the state. It took me about an hour and a half to get home. This was my daily routine. When I came back from work one night at about 11:30, I heard some rumours about labour unrest. The news spread quickly. In front of my apartment, a few neighbours were there talking. They asked me if I had heard the strike news. I said that I had heard rumours, but I didn't know for sure. I went to bed because I was tired. The next day, at about 10:00 a.m., all commercial activity stopped. The grocery store and everything around was closed. The buses stopped, people had to walk. There wasn't a policeman or security officer to be seen anywhere. But there were groups of miners walking toward the coalmine (the biggest one in Valea Jiului). My wife and I joined our neighbours and we started to walk. It was about 11:00 a.m. when we left our block. It took about 20 minutes to walk to the meeting place. It was very strange, because the police had fled from the crowd.

When we arrived, there were 20,000 people: men, women and children, young and old. But the crowd was mostly miners in work clothes. They all had axes on their shoulders. The axe, a primary mining tool, was used for cutting and splitting wood. Most of the miners looked angry, as if they were ready to fight. This mine was the largest of all the mines in Valea Jiului. Millions of tons of coal were extracted from it yearly. I tried to find out what was going on, and discovered that the communist government had changed the miners' retirement plan. A miner normally retires at 58. The new law required 7 more years of work, until the age of 65, for all miners. The immediate cause of the strike was that more than 20 miners had their pension benefits stripped from them. The government changed the law because they were short-handed and needed more labourers, and this small group of 20 men had instigated the strike against the communist regime. The people spread the news to all of Valea Jiului. Buses came one after another, full of miners, women and children, to the city. They came there for justice.

The night shift at the Lupeni mines was staffed with about 5,000 to 8,000 people. When all these miners emerged from the mines at the end of their shift and saw what was going on, they, too, refused to work. So, that is how it started. And, at about 2 p.m. on the second day, I was part of a crowd which had grown to 40,000 people. Everything was happening quickly. The head of the strikers was a young miner who lived in the city of Vulcan. He knew our labour rights very well and he stood up to speak for us. He was a married man with two small children. He took the responsibility to answer and lead the angry crowd. The government yielded. They promised food and to change the working hours from 8 to 6 a day. The retirement plan was to be reinstated. Ration coupons were to be issued, because lots of families couldn't eat well. The strike leaders prepared a new labour agreement. The crowd requested that the president (Nicolae Ceausescu) be present to negotiate for the government. Lupeni communist party officials came instead, to try to stop the strike. But the miners took them and locked them up, and gave them coal to eat and water to drink. They were confined for 3 days, until the president showed up. They required the president to come in person to the mine; no security or policemen. Most of the time policemen were everywhere with guns, but not during the strike.The place where the people congregated was at mine number two. It was on the road which came from the centre of Lupeni. The second gate was where the miners entered to work. The company had a concrete fence about 2.5 metres high. The gate was made of strong metal and it had a small tower for the watchman. That tower was the centre of the strike. From its top, the strike leaders spoke to the crowd. To get to the top of the platform there was a metal ladder. In that tower were the hostage Communist Party officials, about 6 men. People swarmed everywhere. On top of the buildings, trees, roads, and inside the company! Everyone got closer to the tower so they could hear and see better. The place truly was unpleasant for President Ceausescu; no applause or flowers. The people remained there until the third day. Their numbers increased dramatically. They stood there all night and day, seeking better treatment. Changes had to take place. The people were ready to confront the government for the changes. It meant a better life for their families. Whole families participated. I have never seen such unity of the Romanian people. They shared their food so the strike could continue. Lots of sacrifices were made to put President Ceausescu out of office. Some people were advocating his replacement. The people were full of anger, but waited patiently for his arrival for the first two days of the strike. They didn't know what to expect, but they did not budge from that place.

Finally, the heads of the strike decided to go to Bucharest and bring the president to the mine. The preceding day he had promised to come to the mine, but it was a lie. So, on the third day, 80,000 strikers decided to take the train to Bucharest to bring him back. When that news made it to Bucharest, finally he came. He truly didn't know what to expect there. The road to the company was packed. It was so full you could not pass through the mass of people. At about 11:30 a.m., I heard the announcement that "the president has come!" What excitement there was in my heart. I had waited many hours because it was in my interest. I dreamed and hoped things would change for the better.

Suddenly I saw 4 small, black cars trying to come through the crowd. Nobody knew which car the president was in, because the windows were completely black. The people started to move left and right to make room for the cars. But when the cars got in the midst of the crowd they were blocked. They stopped. It was well before gate number two. The security agents got out of the cars to protect the president. But as he got out, the miners formed a wall. Only the president was allowed to walk to the centre of the crowd. All security agents where left behind and not permitted to come forward. Oh, what excitement inside of me, especially to see the liar all by himself. I was tired of his name. There, in that place, the people were angry. That day, President Ceausescu got no flowers or red carpet. He got angry miners who were ready to hurt him. A lot of miners wanted to kill him, but other miners would not permit that. When the crowd saw President Ceausescu, they started to yell at the tops of their lungs. Some of them yelled, "He took our farms," and they said many bad things about him. There were many unpleasant words. And no other Communist Party members were there. Finally, I saw him, at a distance of 50 metres. I saw him perfectly. A grey-headed old man with a wrinkled face, about 1.60 metres tall! He wore a black suit. He walked trembling by the crowd saying, "Don't hurt me." I just thought, in my heart, this is the man who authored all the disasters in this country. This is the man who turned the country upside down. Oh, there were so many questions in my heart, because I didn't understand so many things. Many times, I asked myself what had happened to this country and why it was in turmoil. And it wasn't just me thinking that way. The strikers shared their desires before President Ceausescu showed up.The miners walked him straight to gate number two, about 100 metres from where he got out of his car, to the tower. When they got to the tower, they helped him climb the metal steps until he reached the top. What a sight to see a famous president like him with the common people of Romania. At the top of the tower were the strike leaders and President Ceausescu. The tower was 3 metres high. There, the president delivered his speech. He had one microphone in front of him. The circumstances were obviously not to his liking, but what could he do? After the crowd got quiet, President Ceausescu introduced himself. The crowd started to yell again, but this time with hatred and anger. Ceausescu projected a bad attitude to the crowd and answered very harshly. Then one of the strike leaders standing with Ceausescu stopped the crowd from yelling and read the miners' demands. There were the issues of food, retirement benefits, and changing the working hours from 8 to 6 a day. The miners wanted many of the rights and benefits the Communist Party members got: an increase in salary, one hot meal before work, free hospitals to be re-established and supplied like before, freedom in the country, the punishment of the security agents and policemen for breaking the law, and many more things. Well, he agreed with all the points and questions raised. Surprisingly, his answer was "yes" to all the issues. At about 5.00 in the afternoon, the strike was broken and everybody went home.

We waited for the promised changes. We expected food and better services and better government. I waited to see the things, which were promised and approved by President Ceausescu. I looked for the first truck with meat, cheese, or eggs. I had forgotten how eggs or chicken tasted. Everyone expected changes. Everyone talked of a better life.

We truly expected everything to be just like in the past. But nothing happened. About two weeks later, still nothing had been done. Then we realized the president had lied again. He had left Valea Jiului with empty promises. This wasn't the first time. The only change that occurred was that state security tightened quickly. Eventually, the work programme changed from 8 hours to 6 hours a day. And the retirement plan got increased benefits. Also, the miners got their one free hot meal before work. The food contained meat with vegetables. That meal makes a lot of difference and the food was excellent. This free meal was supported by the government, only for miners who worked underground. But no other promises were kept. Ceausescu promised he would increase the salary, but that was another lie. That was all Ceausescu changed. The grocery stores remained "empty". There were also no hospitals and no supplies. The doctors and hospital staff became discouraged. Then the real nightmare began.

The police started their investigations. Many people were tortured, beaten, "disappeared," and even killed. The communist regime turned like an animal against the people. The head of the strike disappeared, along with his whole family. It wasn't just him; others disappeared, too. People disappeared overnight and nobody knew why. That's how President Ceausescu responded to the people. At night, trucks showed up pretending to help people move, and then nobody saw them again. That's how the security service responded. The cities in Valea Jiului were in a very critical condition, even worse than in the past. I lost all hope. It was a big disappointment for all the people of Valea Jiului. What was to happen to the next generation? There was depression and worry about the future. The Communist Party had seized control of everything local and they were in close coordination with the Romanian state authorities. Anything suspicious, they told the police. Angry communists continually oppressed the common citizens around them. This time, Ceausescu made sure there was no rebellion. He retaliated brutally for his rough treatment at the mine. People barely survived, and nobody cared. You could not trust anybody any more. Everything was worse. President Ceausescu never came back to Valea Jiului. He knew he wasn't welcome. But he never quit hating the miners of Valea Jiului for humiliating him, and we paid until his death with our misery.

The Green Machine

AFTER NINA AND I MARRIED, her family invited us to go to church with them to enjoy worship as a family. I accepted. I had gone to church as a child, but I hadn't known the meaning of it. There, the Pentecostal Church was different. I got to meet the pastor and other Christians who belonged to that church. Some of the young boys and girls were already my friends, but I didn't know they attended the church. They were secret Christians, I guess! I started to go more often, but my heart wasn't in it.

In the summer of 1979, I received my army induction notice. I was 22. At the age of 20, every young boy was conscripted. The period of service was one year and 4 months. So, I presented myself to the army department in Petrosani. Nina, my wife, and brother-in-law, Nelutu, came with me. Before I knew it, I was on the train for the city of Hunedoara. The training base was suburban. When we got there, we stopped at the gate. I heard proud talk from other soldiers who had come to meet us. The camp was fenced with concrete. The wall was 2.5 metres high, but I was used to that. I saw the dormitory and commandant's offices. They were built from very cheap wood, and painted a light blue. My group was about 30 men, from the same part of the country. Most of us knew each other. Anyway, the first thing they did was take us to a big shower, where we changed to military clothes and had our heads shaved. After our shower we got our green army clothes, a heavy leather belt, and a pair of black boots and other clothes. After all that, a lieutenant took us to the mess hall. The food wasn't bad, but there wasn't enough. Romanian people eat a lot of bread. Most of our food contained pasta, rice, potatoes and beans, but not much meat. After that we were shown our barracks. We lined up and our lieutenant talked to all of us for several hours. He told us what was permitted or not permitted in the camp, as well as our purpose in the army. I realized he was very patriotic and belonged to the Communist Party. But that was him. I truly disagreed with him in many ways. I felt that one could be patriotic without being in the army. Anyway, after two hours he showed us to the beds which awaited us.

Our dorm was made from very cheap wood. The toilet was disgusting, but what army toilet isn't? We had metal beds, cotton mattresses, two black blankets, two white sheets, one pillow, and a concrete floor. It didn't matter how much we washed the concrete floor, it stayed dirty. We went to bed about 11pm that night. At 5 o'clock in the morning everybody had to get up, wash their face, shave, and shine boots. After all that, we had to line up to go to breakfast. At 7:30 a.m., all the soldiers had to be in formation for inspection. Then the colonel walked among us from platoon to platoon. There were about 400 soldiers altogether. Ours was a work camp. We had a period of 40 days training. There were no exceptions or excuses. At about 8:30, we walked out from the base to a training area. After 4 hours of running and calisthenics we were very tired. We became very angry with our lieutenant because he made us do more than we were required to do. I knew all the training orders, but the lieutenant thought they weren't tough enough so he added more drills. This training was without a rifle, or any kind of weapon. Thank God he didn't have one. We were sweaty and dirty because of fresh rain. Mud was all over our clothes and boots. Around lunch time, we went back to the base and, after we had eaten, we had two hours to rest. At 3 p.m., we were back in the training area for another two hours. At 5:30 p.m., we returned to the base and went straight to our dorm, cleaned our boots and dried our clothes. We had only one extra change of clothes. At 7 p.m. we ate. At 8 p.m. we were back in our barracks, talking and writing letters to our families. That was our daily routine. During that time, my wife was pregnant and in her fourth month.

Very quickly, I got in trouble with the lieutenant because I went against his rules, especially his teaching about communism. Some of the soldiers accepted his dogma, but I resisted and refused to listen. I was ready to fight. After two weeks, he couldn't put up with me any more. The commander called my wife and tried to talk to her about my attitude. But I didn't change. After three weeks, I was charged with fighting and the army court sentenced me to one year at a disciplinary army base, so I had to do one extra year. Then the army found out from the security forces about my being a part of the miners' strike, so they sent me to do construction work. I was transferred to another platoon, where they worked on big construction projects in the city of Calan. It was about 45 minutes by bus. We had to work from 7:00 a.m. till 6:00

p.m. At 6 o'clock in the morning, we rode the bus to work. By 7:00 p.m. we were back on base. It was all day in the sun, rain, cold and wind for no pay except cheap packs of cigarettes. Our platoon commander talked incessantly of the goodness of President Ceausescu and the communist regime. I never accepted his word and he realized that I was against his teaching. The Lieutenant Commander didn't like it. But he was blind to reality. There was nothing of value in his talk, only lies. All he asked of us was to work hard.

My dear wife came to visit me every month, at the weekend. On Friday afternoon, I was free until Monday morning at 6 a.m. Bulgaru's older brother lived in that same city (Hunedoara), with his parents-in-law, in a state apartment. Gheorghe invited us to stay there for the weekend any time we wanted. Gheorghe showed us gracious hospitality. He asked nothing in return. I was his brother's best friend and we had grown up together. His apartment was very close to the base. Three months later, I was transferred from that base to Valea Jiului in the city of Vulcan (near home). What a joy it was to see myself away from the camp. I felt like I had escaped all that communist propaganda. The new camp was about 3 hours from Hunedoara and Valea Jiului, which was in Petrosani. That new camp had once been a prison. Because of the strike in 1977, lots of miners quit working. The state made the army work underground in the mines in all Valea Jiului.

I heard someone calling my name. I turned around and did a double take. It was my friend, Bulgaru, now also in the army. We hugged each other and talked for a while. He showed me his barracks and introduced me to some of his friends. He had just been recruited and he expected to be transferred to the coalmine in Lupeni (my home). We ate together at the camp canteen. The food was much better than the other camp I had just come from. I stayed two days at the army base. After that, I received new orders. I presented myself to the commander. The base was in the city of Vulcan. The distance between the base and the city where I lived was about 30km. I travelled on the public bus because, as a soldier, the transportation was free for me. In a short time, one of the officers told me that I would be working at the mine in Barbateni. I was excited and very happy, because most of the people there knew me very well. Also, my mother had worked there (repairing electric lamps) for almost 10 years before she became ill. Working underground was no longer problem for me, but my heart wasn't there. I knew I wouldn't last long in that kind of job, but I accepted it for the time being because I wanted to be close to home. All my family were there and I could see them daily. I could spend time with my wife and be around my mother. Before I left the first base, they asked me if I would like to work in a coalmine underground. I knew exactly where the mine was so, of course, I accepted. When I walked into the canteen for the first time, I saw my Aunt Margaretta in the kitchen. Her husband, Aron, had run off with another woman. Margaretta could not have any more children and Aron loved children, so he ran off to find a fertile field. Anyway, when I called her name she turned quickly and, when she saw it was me, she couldn't speak. After many questions, she handed me a big plate of food and walked to the table with me. The canteen was very clean; the tables were covered with white sheets and topped with clear plastic for protection. The floor was made of brown tile and the construction of the building was stronger than the other camp. My Aunt Margaretta was chief cook there. Now food was no longer a problem.

I walked back to the commander's offices and waited until he assigned me to a platoon and to barracks. This base had about 250 soldiers who worked underground. Lots of soldiers went out whenever they wanted to. The most important thing at that camp was the "work". Nothing else mattered much there. One day a week (Monday) was devoted to military training. The other 6 days were for work. My platoon was on the third floor of the barracks. My room had 3 beds, one table and two chairs. On the walls were cheap prints, and there was one big window. In the middle of the room was a big, cheap rug. Very sparsely furnished! For this I was charged 15% of my gross pay.

The very first night there, I went home without permission and spent the night with my wife. She was so happy to see me close to home and having the opportunity to be together. At that time, she was seven months pregnant. The next day I woke up early and returned to camp, pretending that I had slept there. The commanders came to the base at 8 a.m. I had to wait 3 or 4 days until I started working. A few days later, the base commander found out that I was from Lupeni. He asked me what relation I was to Margaretta. I told him she was my aunt.

I kept to myself at the base. I made my army life more private. I didn't fear anyone. In a short time, all the commanders and soldiers all learned of my prior labour strike activity and then they stopped talking to me. I started taking the bus home more frequently. Nobody stopped me. They counted me present for work, even when I wasn't in the camp. The food was good and we had meat at every meal. All the soldiers enjoyed the free hot meal, which we ate together with the civilian miners. Almost every day I was home with my dear wife and mum. Everything was going very smoothly. I had peace for a while, both from the army and within my family. All the commanders knew I was going to work and then riding back home on the civilian bus.

We're All Born Dying

A MONTH LATER I was on third shift. I began coming home earlier because I was very tired. I would go to Nina's parents, because Nina's mother was taking care of her as she was in her ninth month of pregnancy and was expecting a baby boy any day. I was so proud and happy. I wanted to hear a child call me "Daddy". Nina felt the same way, but she was in a lot of pain. She was having a problem pregnancy. Everybody around us was happy and anxious to see the baby. We were poor but happy. I wanted to get special things for Nina and the baby, but money was short. My army pay wasn't much. My wife was very understanding. We were poor and we just had to accept it. It broke my heart that I couldn't do more for Nina. All I could do was wait and pray for the day we could leave Romania.

I came home one morning and Nina awakened and lay beside me. Then, at noon, she woke up again and told me that we needed to go to the hospital! I jumped up and washed my face, and then we left the house. From our house to the hospital was about 5km., but there wasn't any transportation except a hospital emergency ambulance and nobody had a telephone, so we had to walk to the hospital. It was awful to walk all the way, because my wife was already in serious pain. We walked slowly. I held her all the way and tried to distract her from the pain. The last two km. of the walk were in cold rain. We were both crying when we got to the hospital. Nina was vomiting. It was terrible. There was nobody around to drive us. I had no training or experience in caring for a pregnant woman. We would walk about 300 metres and then we would stop to rest. We walked for two and a half hours that way to get to the hospital. When we got to the gate, Nina was completely exhausted and sick. I called the watch woman, who immediately came to the gate with the little gurney. Nina was lying on the asphalt when they arrived. She was too ill to talk. Her pants were soaked. When she left, she turned her head and told me, "I love you". Then she fell unconscious on the journey. One of the nurses asked me from where we had come. I told her and she said, "That's too far to walk." But she understood the situation.

After that, I waited at the hospital entrance for word from the doctor. Later, I was told that my wife was OK and that she had delivered a little boy. What joy filled my heart to know that I had a son. But the lady at the gate told me that the doctor wanted to talk to me, so I went back into my wife's room where she slept. The nurse told me the road that we had walked was too long for her. She said the baby was in a special room. The nurse walked with me to the doctor's office. When I saw him, I recognized him as the father of a girl I had gone to school with. His name was Dr Adesman, a well-known person in that hospital. When I saw him, I knew that something was wrong. We greeted each other and he asked me to sit down. After a few minutes he said, "I am sorry, but I have some bad news for you. Your son's blood supply to his brain is not functioning properly." He was speaking in medical terms, which I didn't understand, so I asked him if there was something wrong with my son. After a few minutes, I asked him to explain it again. Then he said, "John, your son will soon die. He will live no more than 24 hours." When I heard that, I was speechless. Then I asked him if my wife knew, and the doctor said that yes, she did. My heart was broken; I cried for a while and then I asked the doctor if I could see my son. He nodded his head, and asked the nurse to take me to the baby. He was asleep; he looked like a little angel. He had my hair, hands and face, but he had my wife's mouth and nose. I touched him to see if he was still alive.

I questioned in my heart why these things had to happen. Then I remembered what Grandpa had told me about why God allows these things to happen. Then I thought in my heart, if God was a loving God, then surely, he would not let my son die? I know that little children are innocent and ought not to have to suffer and die. All kinds of questions came to me. But the big question was whether God cared.

I wanted to talk this over with my grandpa (Glava). I did not want to have anything to do with a God who would take my son. On the other hand, I wanted to know what my wife thought and felt about all of these things.

It was hard for me to comprehend that my son was born dying. I thought it was so cruel. I would not get to hear him call me Daddy. How I wanted to hear him say that word.

At home, all of the family was waiting to see our son. I knew that my wife and I would be blamed for his death. They would say it was the product of a bad marriage. I knew that it would only add to the pain that Nina was feeling.

All my dreams vanished. I stayed with my son for an hour and just watched him. I longed to hold him in my arms. "Little John" was what we named him. I was so heartbroken that we were not going to get to see him grow up, and he would not get to know us. He was sleeping so very peacefully, but soon he would be leaving us. We would give away the few clothes that we had bought for him. I walked out from my son's room, and went in to my wife's room. She was also asleep. I leaned over her and kissed her on the cheek. Then I went outside to be alone.

The nurses knew the situation and were very compassionate. They tried to comfort me, but I knew that there was nothing Nina or I could do to help our son. That was the most helpless feeling I have ever had.

I knew that afternoon I had to go back to the base. I did not want to leave my wife and son. I stayed a little while longer with Nina. We were silent – there was nothing that we could say to each other. We just held each other and cried.

The nurse told me that Nina would have to stay in the hospital for a couple of days, so she would be able to get her strength built up. I told her that I would go home and tell the family the bad news.

I went to tell my mother first, but she already knew. She was heart-broken. She was hoping to get to see Little John and hold him in her arms and rock him. One of the nurses lived next to my mother and had already told her about the baby. There were no adequate words. Then I went to tell Nina's mother and dad and the rest of the family, especially Grandpa. I truly wanted to know what he would say after all this, so I left and got a bus to go to their home.

When I walked into their house, my mother-in-law looked at me and asked, "John, what's wrong?" I told her about the baby dying and what caused it. After that, I went to see Grandpa and told him about the baby. I didn't want to talk about it, and I didn't ask questions about the meaning of the baby's death.

That evening, I went to the base and told my lieutenant about the situation. He understood, and gave me a 3-day pass. I went back to my mother-in-law's house and, when I got there, my father-in-law was there. He tried to comfort me. We talked for a while, and then I went to bed. I got up early the next day and went to the hospital to be with my wife. When I got there, she told me the bad news about our baby. She said that he had died at about 5 o'clock that morning.

The news spread and soon, all of our family and friends knew it. One of our uncles made a small casket for the baby. My brother-in-law (Nelutu) stayed with us. We didn't talk much. He understood the situation... At about 10 a.m., I took my son and put him in the little casket.

Then we took him home. All of our family got to see our baby. My granny said the baby was like an angel praying for his mother and daddy. I didn't understand what she had said, but I didn't want to hurt her feelings. I knew she loved and cared for me.

That afternoon, we buried him in the cemetery. We made a little hole and placed his little casket in it, and covered it with dirt. We marked his grave with a cross; I put his name on it. Afterwards, we sat in total silence; my wife's sister (Lidia) stayed with us. By about 5 o'clock, everything was done. At 6 p.m., we left the cemetery.

Then, that evening I went back to the hospital to visit my wife. She was feeling much better and she had got her strength back. The doctor said she could go home the next day. The next morning, I was back at the hospital at 7 a.m.; the doctor had released my wife.

The state paid all the hospital expenses. Nina and I walked home with emptiness in our hearts. Our joy had turned to sadness. We had been so excited. Early on I had promised my wife that, when we returned from the hospital, I would carry the baby in my arms. Well, I had, but in a casket. Such an unexpected, deep sorrow left us numb to our souls.

We went to Grandpa, but we were too hurt and confused to know what to ask him. He knew how we were hurting inside. He told us that our son was with Jesus Christ, but we wanted little John with us. It wasn't time for him to be with Jesus. We wanted to hold him in our arms. We wanted to watch him grow. No one should suffer losing a child to death.

An Escape from Communism to a Prisoner of Christ

We were not sure that we ever wanted to try to have any more children. Then we changed our minds, because we did not feel complete. Children make a family. We decided to focus on the future. After my service time was up, we would think about children again. I went on and finished serving my time in the army.

More Death - "And Flights of Angels Sing Thee to Thy Rest"

EVENTUALLY, THERE WAS A PEACE that came into my heart. One day, I came home from work and my wife said she had some bad news for me. She said that our grandpa had died. Glava was Grandpa's name; he was my very best friend.

When I went back to work, I told my commander and I asked for a 3-day pass. My heart was broken all over again. Our grandpa had gone to be with the Lord Jesus Christ. My wife and I immediately went to Grandpa's house, and we learned that he had died of a heart attack at about 10 a.m. My grandpa was the only one who really showed any interest in me. I could share my heart openly with him, and he would teach me. He understood, and never put me down. I have never had a friend like him again. He had grown to mean so much to me. I will always miss his love, compassion and kindness. I can still hear him talking to us and telling us that he was praying for us. Such love he showed to us. I will always remember the warm hug and handshake that he gave me each time we met.

It was another loss that I couldn't comprehend. As we walked to his house, there were so many memories that came to mind. I remember he told me that Jesus Christ loved me. The memories flooded. Once again, Nina and I were lost for words. Our hearts were broken and we felt the great loss. We walked side by side, holding hands and crying. Our life would be so empty without the baby and Grandpa.

I knew that all the family would suffer the loss of Grandpa; he was the centre of all of our hearts and lives. He held the family in unity. He had encouraged every one of us. Any time that any one of us had a problem, we would go to him. He was more than a father to all of us. He was our oracle. We consulted him on all of our plans. He was a man of vision and strength. We all loved him very much. I finally understood what he had been telling me: "I will go to be with Jesus Christ, when I have finished my task that God has given to me to do." Grandpa had truly gone to be with the Lord Jesus Christ, just as he said he would.

His funeral was big. When we got through the mob, we went to the room where he lay in a beautiful casket. My wife's parents, Margaretta and my granny were around the casket. Most of the family was there.

I looked into his face; he looked so peaceful. He looked as though he was asleep; he had a smile on his face. I bade him farewell, but not the sweet memories. I will always have those memories. His love lives inside of me. I long to hear his loving voice! He speaks to me still.

My poor grandma said, "Don't leave me here, please take me with you!" They had been married for 55 years. Grandpa was 74 years old when he went to be with the Lord. Granny was two years older than he was. Her very best friend, her sweetheart and her husband, was no longer with her. She didn't want to go on without him; he had been her whole life. She lived by herself until the end of her life. She was short and skinny, with grey hair and brown eyes, and always had a smile. She was a simple woman, who loved God and people. She talked about Jesus Christ all the time. Every place she went, she knew that Jesus was with her.

Grandpa's Pentecostal Church joined us in mourning his death. The men talked about all the good deeds that Grandpa had done. So many flowers! They were everywhere. There was both joy and sadness in the house. There was laughter and lamentation. Above all, there was sharing memories of Grandpa. We sang gospel songs and mourned his death and celebrated his life for 3 days. The choir from Grandpa's church sang beautiful, impromptu hymns. On the third day, it was time to say our final goodbyes and bury him.

We carried the casket to the ceremony. The Lord gave us a beautiful day to say our goodbyes, and that was what Grandpa would have wanted. We nailed his coffin shut. There were more than 200 people who joined with our family. They put him on a horse-drawn wagon and started to walk to the cemetery. In front was Grandpa's cross. After that was a long line of people carrying the flowers (there were more than 50 wreaths). The horse and wagon followed. The wagon was covered with a beautiful rug and the casket laid on top of it. There were flowers all around the casket. After the wagon came Granny, Nelu and Ana. My wife, mother and Margaretta were behind them, and I and all of the rest of the family. We walked slowly. We stopped several times. And then we would start to walk again. It took us an hour to get to the cemetery. After a short graveside service, we buried him; it was 4 p.m. It had ended. The friends drifted off to their homes, and we went back to Granny's house.

I still couldn't believe that my grandpa was gone. The house was not the same without him. I had always been so excited when I went to see him; wanting to know what wisdom he would have for me. Now there was nothing to look forward to. He was the one who had made the house a home that everyone wanted to come to.

And I never saw my granny smile again; she was not satisfied any more. Every day she would go to the grave and cry. Then she would come home. All she wanted to do was go to the grave and to church and back home. She had lost the desire to live. She stopped visiting the family and the family began to disintegrate. We lost the unity that we had when Grandpa was with us. I went to the grave with Granny many times, and we would just sit there and cry. I know how she felt because I, too, missed him very much. My wife and I loved Granny very much, and we never stopped going to visit her.

I continued to work in the same routine. Daily life went smoothly. After another 14 months, the army court got an order to arrest me. They sent me to a disciplinary base for one year because of my prior fight. That sentence had been imposed a year earlier. I thought they had just forgotten about it. Another broken heart! I just wanted to die. My lieutenant. said that I had to present myself to the commander of the base in the city of Petrosani. I went straight home and told my wife and the rest of the family that I would be gone a year. They asked me why. I tried to explain the best I could what had happened at Hunedoara camp. My family were speechless. I said my goodbyes to everyone and left the city of Lupeni.

The Communist Regime
Retaliates

I REPORTED TO THE DISCIPLINARY BASE and presented the order to the commander. After a short time, I was sent to the city of Bistrita Nasaud. The city was in the north. I took the train there by myself. I presented myself at the base. I had now been separated from my wife and the rest of my family for a whole year.

The camp was for soldiers like me who challenged the authority of the communist regime. I was there not because of the fight, but because I was against the regime. That was the problem. In all of the bases where I went, the "patriotic leaders" found out quickly about my anti-communist virus. I could change my behaviour, but I could never join the Party. So, I was careful and quiet. I did meet a few men from Lupeni whom I already knew. The base was old and was surrounded by a high wall, but it wasn't big. The offices were stone. The floors were concrete. Many of the interiors were made of stone as well. The base's main gate was made of metal. To the side of it was a visitors' room, where I waited a couple of hours until my papers were processed. When I walked inside, to the right were 6 dorms for disciplinary cases like me. On the other side were barracks for the base's regular staff. The staff watched the base but we had no interaction with them. When they were out, we went inside. My dorm was open. Inside were 20 metal beds. I was issued with a mattress, two black blankets, two sheets, one pillow and another change of clothes. The base was very clean, the food was good, but there was no work on the base. We all spent most of our time in our dorms, outside on benches, or on the grass. It wasn't bad, but the time went so slowly because there was nothing to do.

I missed my wife and family. That was the whole purpose; to separate us from our families. That was the punishment for us. While I was there, my wife had got a job with a company that made clothes. The pay was not good, but it helped to pay the bills. We wrote to each other. She let me know what was going on at home. I knew that she didn't have the money to come to see me, but she did send me cigarettes. Also, every 3 months, she sent me a 3-kg package of food and sweets.

The commanders were indifferent to us. Once a week we had training, then the rest of the week we lay back. I had to stay there for 6 months, then they transferred me to another base.

The new base was in another city, which was Caracal. That city was in the region of Oltenia. The reason they transferred me was because the base was full. There were 50 other soldiers transferred for the same reason. Two lieutenants escorted us. We travelled all night. They didn't shackle us; we walked freely. I didn't look for trouble any more. I planned to go home as soon as possible and to be with my wife and family. I had only 6 months left.

When I saw the new base, I was excited. It was a big base and it had a lot of room to walk. It was surrounded by a wire fence. Everything was separate: the commander's offices, dormitory, kitchen, showers and library. There was a lot of space that they didn't use. I spent a lot of time walking and working out; I did a lot of weight-lifting, and spent most of my time by myself. There was no church on the base. There was no one who had a Bible. I forgot all about God. The commanders were a joke, because they didn't care about anything. Their speech was very eloquent, but their actions weren't. They weren't interested in us. The time went slowly. I tried to find an occupation.

My wife and I kept in touch. I knew she worried about me. I wanted to let her know that everything was alright. She was already doing a lot for me. Also, I knew she wanted to come to visit me but she didn't have the money. I truly understood her situation. When I had 3 months left at the disciplinary base, my wife wrote a letter with some very bad news; she said that her dad had been killed in a mining accident. I was shocked and it broke my heart. The commander would not let us receive phone calls, so I found out through her letter. I was not allowed to go to the funeral. I knew that my wife and sisters were without a father. There was Lidia, 15, Margaretta, 12, and Amelia, 11 years old. Their father was the only one who had been working. I worried about them and wondered how they would survive. My mother-in-law didn't work outside the home. It was a sad and hectic time. My wife stayed with her mother. My mother was back in the hospital. We lost the apartment because I was in the army and my wife couldn't pay the bills. Everything was going wrong. The family was falling apart and I could not be of any help. When my father-in-law died, my mother-in-law started having problems with her heart. Her heart deteriorated, and I knew she would be next. I loved her as if she were my own mother. I knew that she would have her wish to go to be with Grandpa soon.

My memories of Grandpa are still fresh. I remember the things that he and Granny did for me. He was proud of me and had not been ashamed to speak to me. Three deaths in our family discouraged us all.

I really started to hate this green uniform. I felt like I had been born in these clothes. I felt that time had stopped. One week later, I got some pictures from my dear wife of the funeral. I cried when I saw the pictures, but there was no one with me to share my grief. That year turned into 5 years But, finally, my time was up; it was the summer of 1981. I got my orders to return to the old base where I had previously been. That meant I got to go home to Lupeni. What joy filled my heart. But there was also sadness because of the loved ones who were dead.

I travelled seven hours by train and bus until I arrived at Petrosani. I presented my papers to one of the commanders. He asked me what I had done. Well, I remained silent. It was about 10 a.m. when I was in his office. He was new and didn't know about me yet. I asked him how long he had been working at the base. He said 4 months. I told him I had lived here in Valea Jiului all my life. When he heard that, there were no more questions. My papers and new orders were ready in one hour. I left the base at 11 a.m. under new orders. I had to report to Lupeni. Three new platoons had moved there while I had been gone.

First, I went to see my wife. I knew she was waiting for me, and I couldn't wait to see her. My mother had been released from the hospital, and had come home. My wife stayed with her to help her. When I got to my mother's apartment and my wife and my mother saw me, they were ecstatic. We all sat down and caught up on all the news. My mother told me all the bad things that had happened, especially about the state authorities. My mother was very worried about me, because she knew I didn't agree with the Communist Party. My mother tried to warn me about them, to stay away from them. I wasn't afraid, but I was concerned about my wife and mother and the rest of the family.

All the houses close to Granny, (Aunt Margaretta's and my mother-in-law's) had to be demolished, because of the coalmine running under them. The state was building substitute apartments for the displaced people. There were still 100 more houses to be destroyed. Granny, my mother-in-law and Nelutu got apartments in the same building and on the same level, on the third floor. All 3 apartments were close together. Aunt Margaretta lived with Granny in the same apartment. She was still was working as the chief cook for the army. She took the public bus daily to work. Before that, this neighbourhood had been gypsy camps. The state scattered them and the farmer residents all over the city and that's how the state took their land by force. They cleaned up the area and built a new grocery store and new roads of concrete. When my wife told me all these things, I couldn't believe it; all this happened in one year.

I left the apartment and went to the new base and checked in. It took me only 10 minutes to walk there. There was no fence. The commander took my orders and I waited about an hour. When he came out of his office, he knew my entire history. He told me I wasn't allowed to go to any bars. He also warned me that I should not have another fight. He also knew that this was my home town and he didn't care where I lived as long as I showed up for work. They put me in a room with two other soldiers from the new platoon. They were far away from home. They were both from Moldova. They were about 1000km from their families. I had two months left in the army. I started working the very next day in the same place, underground. Most of the civilians knew me, and there was nothing new for me. There was nothing against me this time, so I went home that very night and changed clothes, and my wife and I went to visit the rest of our family. We went straight to the new apartment complex where our family was placed. That night I got to see Granny, Aunt Margaretta, my mother-in-law, my sisters-in-law and Nelutu with his wife, Maria. All of them lived in 3-room apartments. As I walked through the apartments, I noticed that they were shoddy. They already had problems with the plumbing. They had hot water only once a week. The electricity and water were cut off from 10 a.m. till 4 p.m. The store was beautiful, but there was nothing to buy in it.

When I came home from work I would change clothes, and Nina and I would walk everywhere. We visited my Aunt Victoria, and what a joy it was to see her again. She cried when she saw me back home. The time went fast and my army time finished quickly. I knew I had to face life and take responsibility as the head of the family. I had acquired no job skills in the army. I was resentful about that. I had given several years to the state but developed no skills. They fed and clothed me and used me to do manual labour. I felt like I was doing them a favour without pay. I had been ready to study and learn, but there had been no substantial skill training, just communist indoctrination. My army service was of no benefit to me or Romania. It was just painful separation from my family. It was without purpose.

Lupeni – Back to the Mines

I WALKED HOME AFTER I was discharged from the army. It was the end of the summer of 1981. I came home without money, clothes or other provisions.

I had to apply for a job immediately. This time I was hired at the Lupeni mine to work underground. Nina quit her job because I made enough money to take care of all our needs. This time our families helped us a little. They helped us with food and a place to live. I kept my job and caught up on some of our bills, especially what we owed our family and our neighbours.

We stayed with our family. Mother was in the hospital for cancer treatment in Bucharest. Christmas was near and we were struggling. We spent our Christmas with our family, but I couldn't shoulder my part of the expenses. We didn't have much food, because the whole country was suffering from a lack of basic necessities. Our wages were not sufficient to cover all our expenses.

After all the holidays, the state accepted my application for an apartment. There was a new location where lots of apartments were opening. Because I had a hazardous job in the coalmine underground, the state gave me special consideration. The apartment was close to where my wife's family lived. We were very close to Granny, my mother-in-law, my sisters-in-law, Aunt Margaretta and my brother-in law, Nelutu. Our new apartment had two bedrooms, a small kitchen, a bathroom, small hall and a big balcony in front. The bedrooms had red carpet. There was just enough room for my wife and me, temporarily. The apartment had very large windows, except the bathroom window, which was small and was at the rear of the apartment. I knew a few neighbours, because we worked in the same place. My wife and I lived there for 5 years. The apartment had a beautiful view in the front. We could see the elementary school and the grocery store. The River Jiul flowed beside our apartment. On the right side was a very high hill of rocks and forest. That hill was 100 metres high. From it I could see all the new developments. It was a beautiful view, I could see everywhere. And we climbed that hill many times, just for recreation.

All the neighbours knew one another. All the men worked in the coalmine, underground. Many times, I became angry with myself and God. I asked my wife, "Why doesn't God help us?" She said, "I don't have any answers to your question." Because of this, we both stopped going to church and reading our Bible for several years. I had one Bible that my grandpa gave me before he died. It just lay there on the table, unopened.

The whole city of Valea Jiului was a disaster. The state authority became more abusive. The country was falling apart under communism. Eventually, there was nothing left. I told my wife, "There is a better life than this." My wife agreed with me, but she didn't understand the consequences, and I didn't want her to know.

It was time to leave the country. It was the summer of 1982; I went to work on the second shift. My work shift was 6 hours, due to the strike in 1977. The 6-hour shifts persisted for several years. In 1982, I heard many rumours that the government was going to change the hours back to 8-hour shifts. When I heard that, I knew immediately that they could not do that again because the state made a binding agreement to 6-hour shifts. That included the whole mining industry. The law was very clear. And, for that reason, I resisted, and I was naive; I didn't know that the law could be changed. I remember the strike from 1977 changing a lot of things. I also knew that a lot of miners disappeared afterwards, but it didn't stop there.

One day, when I went to the shower after work, there were a lot of people, young and old, ready to stop work. It was frightening. One of my friends asked me if I had heard what the regime's latest plans were. Then he said that his co-workers wanted to know if I would be the strike leader. Everyone was looking to me, but I knew I couldn't accept. They continued to make strike preparations. I knew I was in danger. I knew that the state would kill me if I was involved in a labour strike again. I knew how the state worked. They already knew that I had been a part of the 1977 strike. Even a rumour would be fatal. When I left the company, I went home.

When I got to the apartment, I told my wife what had happened at the company. I told her about being asked to lead the strike. She started to cry. She said, "John, we are going to be in so much trouble because of that." I told her that I walked out without responding one way or the other. We went to bed. It was 1 a.m. At 7 a.m., the doorbell rang. When my wife looked through the peephole, she told me it was the police. They had already heard! I jumped up and saw two police cars. I didn't know how to escape. We lived on the third floor. I went into the bathroom and wriggled out of the small window. I could reach my neighbour's balcony. From there, I dropped from balcony to balcony until I reached the ground, then I ran another 300 metres to safety. After all that, I waved to my wife to let the police in. All this took only a few minutes. Fear breeds haste. I ran to the closest hill. When I got to the top, I stopped. I could see everything that was going on at the apartment. Security agents were everywhere. They were very agitated. Then I realized the danger. I sat there and watched. More cars came. The authorities walked up and down the streets. Some of them stayed there and the rest left. They looked on top of the building. Every 10 minutes they would meet and talk. They looked around all the apartments. I watched them from a safe distance. After 4 hours they all left. Civilian authorities were everywhere. I knew most of them. I couldn't go back to work any more. That afternoon, I secretly returned to my apartment. When my wife saw me, she was speechless. Later on, she asked me how I got back, because the police were everywhere. I told her that I saw everything from the top of the hill. We sat down and talked. We came to the conclusion that I hadn't done anything against the state, so we decided to stand up for our rights.

Prison, But No Penitence

THAT EVENING, THE DOORBELL RANG. I opened the door and two civilian policemen were there. I said, "Yes? What are you all looking for?" One of them, who knew me, said that he had searched for me all day. They told me that I had to come to the police station to tell them about what had happened the day before. They put me in the police car and took me to the main police station at Valea Jiului, (the city of Petrosani). They quickly put me in jail. It was 10 p.m. when I was taken to court. No one was in the courthouse but me and 10 policemen. There they asked me for the names of the others from the strike group. The state had the names of strikers – including me. I had resisted by running. Within 4 hours I had been sentenced. It was so fast that I had no idea what was going on until I arrived at prison. I was persecuted because I asked for my labour rights. The state's answer was prison. They locked me up for 6 months for illegal labour activities. The same night, after sentencing me, the policemen took me to prison. I was once again behind a huge metal gate. One of the policemen handed some papers in at the gate and, in 10 minutes, we were inside the prison. This was the first time I had heard of Bircea Prison. It was close to the city of Deva. My Aunt Victoria had moved to Deva, but I didn't know her address. Anyway, one of the prison officers came and asked me if I knew why I was there. I said, "No, sir," and asked what the charge was. He looked up and then looked at me. I waited for his answer. In a few moments he shook his head and said, "You are here for instigation." I said, "What does that mean?" Then the officer looked through some papers and put me in one room by myself. About an hour later, one of my friends who worked with me stepped into the room. When we saw each other, we laughed. I said, "What are you doing here?" (I knew he was part of that group, too). He said, "John, someone gave our names to the state authorities." I had no idea how the police had come to my door earlier that morning, and knew my name. We realized that someone in our group was working for the state police.

The prison was a massive building in the shape of a "U", with two floors. It was concrete with iron bars. In the centre was a big plateau made from concrete. Every morning, the prisoners lined up there for work. On top of the walls were watchtowers. The guards in the towers carried rifles.

The prison wing held 100 men. There were big windows and bars outside. The beds were metal, stacked 4 high. But where my friend and I were housed, there were two-bed cells. They gave us cotton mattresses, sheets and pillows. The cell had a concrete floor, a toilet and one window with bars. That was all the room contained. One thing they allowed was the *Scinteia Tineretului* newspaper. It was primarily about the president of Romania – Ceausescu – and his wife, and their travels. They also provided political propaganda, which nobody read. All we could see was what was the inside of the prison. We were not allowed to look out of the window. The entrance door was maple with metal bars. It was about 10cm thick. The entrance door had a slot for food. Once a week, we left our cell when we took showers or visited. We sat in our room for 24 hours a day, 7 days a week. We meditated a lot.

They fed us 3 times a day. Breakfast was two slices of bread and black coffee. Lunch was cornflower mixed with water and a bowl of soup (beans, cabbage, rice, potatoes, beets, eggplant or leaves). The soup had no vegetables in it – nothing but water, boiled chicken bones, or pig's feet. At night we got one bowl, with pasta or potatoes with different kinds of leaves in it which I did not recognize. And it was bitter. At night time they gave us a bowl of boiled grain. No meat or any sweets. Anyway, the food was terrible and the outside supplies from family weren't enough. I was hungry all the time. Sometime the guards cut our rations, saying that we were undeserving. Their attitude was very cruel. My grandma at the farm fed her hogs better than we were fed. But we were hungry and had to accept it. The prison approved gift packages with food, but that was only 5kg every three months. They also allowed 15 packs of cigarettes every 3 months. They also provided one toothbrush, one tube of toothpaste and one bar of soap; and that was it! A visit was permitted once every 3 months. We were allowed only a 40-minute conversation on a telephone through a glass window, with only one person. The prison did not provide prisoners with resources for hygiene. Clothes weren't much, only the necessities that the state provided. The uniform that I wore daily was white and grey. We had black boots and a few underclothes. I was always cold, because of the temperature and the concrete construction. I never thought there was such a place in my country. Angry guards were cruel. They enjoyed beating prisoners. Many prisoners died there. No medical assistance was provided, except for serious injuries and emergencies, and then only at the last moment. Several weeks into my stay there, my friend and I were in maximum security; I asked myself why, what had we done? We were kept in the same room for a month and were unable to communicate with anyone except the guards who fed us.One night, quite by surprise, we were moved to a new, larger dormitory containing over 100 political dissidents. Some were there for active anti-regime activities. Others were there for sedition of varying degrees, ranging from the errant, unwise comment made in a public place (and overheard), to writing anti-regime propaganda. My friend's political crime was "presence", merely overhearing the rest of us. He "listened" when he should have run away. Our political "re-education" was to be by forced labour on state farms. We were bussed to the farm, where we worked 12 hours straight. We did this for 5 days a week. The alternative to work was to receive a very professionally administered state beating, so the work wasn't so bad by comparison. We were constantly admonished to work harder. Occasionally one of us, at random, was beaten as an example to the others not to slacken off. We were not people any more, we were beasts of burden. I couldn't believe that these things could occur in my country. At the farm, there was a civilian worker who was the manager. He told us what we had to do each day. It didn't matter what the weather was like; hot, cold, rain, wind, we were in the fields working. The first 3 months were warm and weren't so bad, but in November we were miserable. The cold winter winds were horrid. The ground was frozen. The work became harder day by day. We harvested frozen potatoes, carrots, beets, corn and other vegetables, which were left over from the regular harvest season. We had no gloves, and no extra clothes. It was as cold as -20^{0}C. My face was cracked. I could hardly open my mouth. No medicine was allowed, or given to us. I had to move constantly to keep from freezing.

This was our daily routine except for the weekend, when we stayed in the dorm. There was no place to shower after work. I can still remember my wife coming in December to visit me and not recognizing me. She cried. My swollen face was almost unrecognizable. I told her that this was our communist education. We had no words for a few moments – we just looked at each other. I told her that there was no hope for me in Romania any more. I saw no future. She still didn't know what kind of treatment we got inside the institution. We were not supposed to tell anybody outside the walls. That is how we were instructed. But I really didn't care if our conversation was overheard.

Living from Hand to Mouth

IN JANUARY 1983, I WAS RELEASED from Bircea prison. I was destroyed physically and mentally. I was angry, bitter and full of hatred against the state. All these things turned me into a wild animal. This savage experience left me short-tempered and potentially very violent. These changes were deep and profound. So profound that I felt

compelled to conceal them from my wife upon my release. When my friend and I walked together out of that prison, we had nothing to tell anyone. No one could comprehend what we had been through.

My Aunt Victoria moved into the city of Deva. This city was about 20 minutes away. When we got there, my friend walked to the train station to go back to his family in Lupeni. My wife, my brother-in-law and I stayed in Deva for a few days with Aunt Victoria. She was excited and happy to see us. She hadn't expected us but, when she saw me, she cried. We ate and then we talked. I explained to her why they put me in prison. She couldn't believe it, but she knew it was true. My aunt was another big piece of my heart. I got to visit my aunt's daughter and her family. They were all happy to see me out. They knew that I was in prison nearby, but there was nothing they could do for me, because of the rules. They all knew where my heart was.

After two days in Deva, we returned to our family in Lupeni. When I got home, I went to visit Granny, Aunt Margaretta and my mother-in-law. They were very happy to see me back. Thank God no one knew what I had been through. I tried my best to put behind me all those negative things, but they festered inside. My family could tell that I wasn't the same person. They understood enough to never ask me about prison. I didn't have anyone to unburden my anger onto. Later on, I found out that all my financial support was from Nina's mother. I cried. I knew she cared about me, but not like that. My wife stayed with her mother all the time I was gone. The money for the cigarettes, monthly packages, and for the train, was all from her. When I found out, I didn't have the words to thank her. My mother-in-law had only a small state pension to support her after her husband died in an accident. She also had 3 little girls (Nina's sisters) at home to support. My brother-in-law had helped my wife, too.

When I came back, I had to report to the police in Lupeni. Those were the rules, by law. The police were not pleased that I was back. They made sure that I couldn't go back to the mines. I made a lot of applications for a job at the same position, but the state mining company refused all my applications from the beginning. I asked the personnel office what was going on. One of the employees said, "John, we cannot hire you in this company any more, since you have been associated with the 1977 strike and have gone to prison for your anti-communist attitude and statements." In my own country, I was no longer free to work where I desired. They wanted me to leave the mine premises immediately. I didn't realize that, after my imprisonment, I was considered dangerous by the mining company. Many of my old friends from the job didn't want to talk to me any more. While I was there, I found out that my friend (from prison) had left the city of Lupeni and gone back to his home town. I never saw him again. He realized that there was no hope for him in Lupeni but, in my case, Lupeni was my home. Where could I go? I tried another mining company in a nearby city, but they refused my application too. Being in prison wasn't enough for the communist regime. They ordered all the companies from Valea Jiului not to hire anyone who had been in prison. I was the black sheep. I didn't argue with the little people, because I knew the true source of my persecution.My financial and social situation got worse. I felt like there was no place for me in that city. My family was very concerned about me and my wife. Even my friends had nothing new to talk about, except my financial situation. I hated it. I got to the point that I could not trust anybody any more. We were reduced to borrowing money from our relatives and some friends who understood and remained loyal to us. After a while, we couldn't pay it back. I remember that bill-collectors came to ask for money we owed. My wife and I were quiet in the apartment and pretended we weren't at home, until they left. So, I got many different menial jobs in different places... temporary! Whenever the security service discovered where I was working, I was fired. I was fired without reason. I was told only, "We don't need a trouble-maker." So, I had to move on – we decided to look in other cities for jobs. My wife and I were in bad shape. We bounced back and forth for a while between our relatives on both sides, city to city. That didn't last long.

I remember when I found a job 100km from my home, in the forest, cutting trees. I worked on a tractor. In the back of the tractor were two cables, with which I pulled the trees to the place where we lived, and from there they were carried by big trucks to the lumber company. That was the longest job (6 to 7 months) I had in that period. The state security service lost track of me during that time. They thought I had left the city, which I did during the week. I was home only at weekends. I didn't enjoy that job because it didn't pay well, but I had to accept it because of our bills. Nobody knew where I worked, except our relatives so, when I came home on weekends and if a policeman asked where I worked, I would answer that I hadn't found a job yet. To get to work from our apartment, I had to take a bus, a train and finally drive the tractor to the forest where I worked during the week. After the work week, I drove the tractor to the train station and left it in the parking lot. Nobody bothered it because it was state property. The people around got to know me well, but I didn't show my face to any policemen. When I returned for the next week's work, I had to drive about 30km. It was a country road and there were lots of hills and curves, but it was a very quiet place. I often heard the birds singing, and saw them flying from tree to tree. The forest work camp was beautiful. There was a house with 3 rooms. One big room was for the workers. There were several men who slept there. Those people were from Moldova. They specialized in wood-cutting. Their families stayed at home. The second room was for our supervisor and his wife, but they didn't stay there with us. The supervisor came with his wife only when he had to pay us. He may have come to the mountain to deliver spare parts for our chainsaws or my tractor when we needed them. He was a privileged communist.

I slept in the third room. It had one big bed. Sometimes my dear wife would join me, but she couldn't stay long because of the rugged conditions; no electricity, water or toilet was provided. The men washed their clothes in a small basin and dried them by hanging them in the woods. There was a clear, cool, mountain stream. This company also had its own store, which provided food weekly. So, once a week, we shopped for groceries. Our food was canned vegetables, fat back, bread and other staples. We worked long hours, especially in good weather. It was hard and dangerous work, especially after the rain because everything was slippery around the tractor. We started work early in the morning and stopped at dark. There was no time to cook. Then, in a short time, I moved on because of our finances. Our relatives never gave up on us. They supported my wife most of the time.

It was two months until Christmas 1983. I decide to stay home for the holidays and to spend time with Nina. After the holidays, my mother became ill. I felt that she was near the end. She became weaker day by day. She couldn't stand up or walk for longer than two or three minutes. I could see in her face that she had lost all hope. My mother didn't complain about her pain. She told us that she had to go back to Bucharest in the spring to see the doctor. She had already had two major surgeries there. Meanwhile, I was still job-hunting. I put in a lot of applications, but to no avail. I only wanted to cover our expenses and pay back what we owed our relatives. I was very depressed because of our situation, and it got worse every day. Even our best friends stopped inviting us to visit them. I decided to move on and to look for something better elsewhere, so I left my wife and went to Constanta, on the Black Sea. I had heard that the stevedores there made good money. I knew it was hard work, but I was accustomed to that from the coalmines. I had been enlightened about the good-paying dock work by Dorel, a friend of mine in the next apartment block. We met there and we became good friends. He explained to me lot of things about the port city of Constanta. He also told me that I may have the opportunity to leave Romania on a commercial ship. He explained to me that he had worked there earlier for a period of several years. I realized that he knew everything about that city.

The distance between Lupeni and Constanta was about 1000 km. by train. Dorel and I left one afternoon and went to the train station. I had already said goodbye to my dear wife and the rest of the family. We took very little money and a few clothes. After 10 hours of travelling on the "Express" train, we arrived at the Constanta train station. The train station was huge. It had many platforms. It was red brick and concrete. The floor was red tile. It had huge windows. When we got off the train, we walked through it. When we got to the front of the station, we saw very large streets, which went in all directions. I saw the huge ships floating in the harbour a short distance away. The commercial ships were docked to unload or load their merchandise. It was the first time in my life I had seen such ships. The buildings near the wharves were new and 10 floors high. I was amazed at the beautiful parks. After that, I saw the Black Sea... so much water! To the horizon there was nothing, just water. The waves at the shore were big and noisy. It was the beginning of February 1984 when Dorel and I got there. The temperature was moderate. We were in the south and the temperature wasn't frigid like in my home town. They don't have snow there, only cold rains. The winds shifted; they blew in all directions. We walked quickly to the barracks, which belonged to the Port of Constanta. When we got there, we presented our identification and the personnel office gave us an application for stevedore work. We were informed that, in two weeks, we would get an answer with approval or disapproval. They gave us a room.

The port in Constanta made cheap barracks available for the employees. The stevedores were always working. The company supplied workers with two meals a day for a period of 3 weeks. When we got there, we had to put in our applications for jobs and give our identification papers to the personnel office. The port office gave the information to the police, and the police had to find out all about our personal history. I had never been to this city before. This city was famous for tourists who came from all corners of Europe. There was a beautiful beach on the Black Sea.

The port barracks were warm. The water and electricity were always "on." We had a room with a heater and good, clean blankets and sheets. There was a hill close to the barracks, from which we could see most of Constanta. I often sat there, on top of the city. The big ships were imposing. The port was almost a separate city. I looked at the harbour and the water, and was in awe. I felt very small on this planet. The next day, we walked for a while in the city to see the new sights. There were flocks of street vendors in front of small businesses, selling clothes and shoes. And we wandered around in a big fish market, just to get the feel of the city. Most of the people were Turks and they were not pleasant. Most of the cars were foreign, especially around the hotels. The grocery stores had the same problem as the ones at home – there was nothing in them to buy except fish. Every day I walked on the seashore. My feet became accustomed to the soft sand. I sat down near big tidal rocks, where the seawater came in furiously and hit them. I was enchanted by the sounds of the sea. They were powerful new sounds to me but then, as a country boy, everything here was new and strange for me.

The local dialect was different, too, so I heard, but didn't understand, the street talk. In the city, there was a second sea – a sea of people. The noisy trams could be heard from a distance. But, despite the negatives, Constanta was beautiful. It captured my imagination, if not my heart; I felt I had to move on. My intention was to start work and to send money to my wife as soon as possible. I was very lonely there.

In two weeks, the responses to our work applications came back. Dorel was accepted, but my application was rejected. I couldn't be hired as a stevedore in Port Constanta. I didn't bother looking for other jobs there, because I knew I had no chance. I had to return home. Dorel wouldn't stay without me. Now there remains nothing in my memory of Constanta except the Black Sea. I can still hear the water and see the waves.

I went back home, broken-hearted, because I could not find a decent job to support my wife. I told her and our relatives what had happened. I came to the conclusion that I would never get job because of the communist regime. In the springtime, I found another "undercover" job, at a small company which researched mineral deposits in the mountains. I worked as a mechanic repairing diesel engines. It wasn't good pay, but we survived. I worked there for almost a year. It was near to my apartment and I wanted to stay around home, because my mother was in bad shape.

Burying My Mother

IN SEPTEMBER 1984, MY MOTHER went to the hospital in a critical condition. I went with her this time, by small car. A week later, she died. It had been her third surgery for cancer, but the tumour had spread all over her body. The hospital was in Bucharest – the capital of Romania – where the doctors with the experience were, but there had been no hope for her. She was 43 when she died. I don't know if she was saved, because she never went to church or read the Bible. She never mentioned or talked to me about the Bible. Even though my wife was with me, I felt truly alone. I had my wife, but I didn't count on her like I had my mother. My situation was so bad that I didn't have money to pay for her funeral, but my relatives and neighbours, and some of our friends, came together and helped me and my wife with the finances. The hospital notified me about her death by emergency letter. They asked me what I was going to do about her body. I said I would come and pick her up and bring her back home. They said they could cremate her at the hospital and save the funeral expenses. I said, "NO, NO; I'll be there in 24 hours." I took my brother-in-law with me and we left at night on the express train. My wife called her Uncle Nelu (who lived in Pitesti) and told him about the situation. She told him to call the regional transportation office for permission to bring my mother home on the train. When my brother-in-law and I got to the hospital, my mother was in the basement, where the cool air was, laid on a concrete table and covered with a white sheet. One of the nurses let me see her. She appeared to be asleep. We brought a casket and took her from there. None of my relatives, friends and especially my neighbours believed it, but everything went smoothly and we made it back. Many people came to my mother's funeral. After 3 days, we took her to her grave and we left her there, forever to rest in peace. I was completely destroyed. My faith in God was gone. I didn't want to hear about God because I didn't see any mercy from him in my life. My mother was now a permanent part of Romania, but I didn't want to be.

Run, Rabbit, Run

IN 1985, I PLANNED TO FLEE Romania. I was going to become an emigrant and run to the West. I was searching for any information I could get about crossing the border. I thought about my plan day and night, and about how to cross the border of Romania into Yugoslavia and not be seen. As I prepared myself for this dangerous adventure, I met a soon-to-be friend, Chris Constantinescu, and he helped me plan my escape. He had just got out of prison himself for being caught illegally close to the border. He had met a lot of people with the same charge. I put my confidence in him, because he knew things better than I did.

The security service suspected I might plan to leave the country and they kept watching me, trying to stop me from leaving. I could no longer walk openly on the streets. Everyone asked me if it was true – that I wanted to leave. I would say to everyone (friends, neighbours, relatives), "Yes". I could not put up with this communist regime any longer. Some of my friends understood, but some became my enemies. Our most trusted friends were the first to avoid us. They lived in fear of the state security forces. They couldn't associate with us. Some of our family turned their backs on us. I truly did not care what they thought about me any more. My wife never opposed me, because we had the same feelings. She told me many, many times, "John; I don't care what the people say about you, I'll be on your side. I know that one day things will change, and something better will come." If one of my friends walked on the same side of the road and we met together, he would cross to the other side to avoid me.

There were many days when we had no food in our apartment. I stole many things to trade for food. Surviving each day became harder and harder. The job I had was insufficient to cover our expenses, but nobody cared any more, especially our friends. They were wilfully blind to our plight, because we were dangerous to them. The fear of communist authority overpowered their other emotions. It wasn't their fault, it was the way the communist regime relied on fear to control the people. My life was constantly in jeopardy. I realized that I was nothing on this earth, just a "stranger". I had nothing to lose. I was without a mother, a father, brothers, sisters, money, or possessions. Of course, I had promised my dear wife that, when I escaped, I would work very hard and send her money so she could catch up with our bills and what we owed to people. Dreams and plans came to me all the time. I could see a better life. My future was full of hope. I felt like I didn't exist for Nina any more. I felt responsibility for my wife, but I believe she understood the situation. She had the same hopes and dreams I had, but it was too dangerous for her to leave. I foresaw many good things to come before I left my country, but I didn't want to lose my wife. We truly loved each other. I wanted to do something more for her. She had been under a lot of stress over me. She had suffered because I did not agree with the communist regime. I refused to change my character from human to wild beast like the Communist Party demanded, so I had no choice but to leave, or die in prison.

My friend Chris and I met daily and discussed the things that needed to be done. When the police authority found out that we were friends, they tried all kinds of tricks to catch us with our own words. We didn't answer their questions. We remained silent when we were harassed at the police station with political questions. We avoided the authorities at every opportunity. My mother had been dead for one year when our plans to escape began to accelerate. I was then attempting to escape for the first of 3 times. In August 1985, I left Lupeni with my friend Chris, on the road to the border. I was really excited. I didn't think of the consequences that might await me. I told my wife goodbye and, with tears in our eyes, we separated once again, not knowing for how long.

Chris and I took the train for a few hours. 40km from the border, we got off the train. We started walking through farm fields, hills and some mountains. We had a small backpack with a little food and a few maps of Romania, Yugoslavia and Austria. We also had a small compass for orientation and binoculars to look around us for troops in the daytime. We waited until August because we would then find fresh vegetables and fruit ready to eat in the fields. Another reason was that the fields were green and helped conceal us. The corn was high enough to walk through without being seen. We had left with very little money in our pockets. After two weeks of walking, we came to a small town about 20km from the Yugoslavian border. We planned to cross the border and go through Yugoslavia on the many un-patrolled country roads. We stayed off the main paved roads – they were too dangerous.

One afternoon while we were walking on a small county road, a big truck came up behind us. It stopped beside us. The driver asked us where we were going. We had no good answer. The driver knew we were strangers in that town. All the local people knew each other. The driver said, "I know you're running away." We remained silent. The locals knew that strangers were usually illegal emigrants. So, when they saw suspicious strangers like us, they called the police. At the time, we didn't realize that the driver would report us. An hour later we looked behind us and saw the truck with the policeman in it. They arrested us. After searching our backpack and beating my friend, they knew exactly what our plan was and what we intended to do. We sat in handcuffs for the rest of the night. The next morning, they put us on a public bus to the local courthouse. There was one officer guarding us. When we got to the courthouse, we saw many armed soldiers and with them many illegal Romanian emigrants, nabbed at the border. I was shocked to see how these people had been beaten. Then I realized the danger. An officer told us to sit down on the hardwood benches until he finished his paperwork. We were still cuffed. Chris was on the right and I was on the left. The guard doing our paperwork left us. He told one of the soldiers to watch us as he walked away. I looked on the concrete floor and saw a paper-clip, which I picked up. I told Chris that we were about to get out of that mess. I bent the paper-clip into a key. Then Chris and I went to the bathroom, where I took the handcuffs off. Then we jumped out of the bathroom window. We found ourselves at the back of the building. We split up; I ran up the hill, while Chris walked around the courthouse into the centre of the city.I ran for about two hours non-stop, with the handcuff on my left hand. The handcuff got very tight around my wrist and my hand turned blue. I stopped and, with the paper-clip, I tried to loosen the handcuff. The pain stopped me from running. After 30 minutes of playing with the paper-clip I finally got it open. Oh, what release I experienced. I rested until I got my strength back again. After another 20 minutes, my hand regained feeling and colour. I was already in the forest, with bushes around me. I knew the worst danger was over. For 3 days I sat in one place, not moving. Then I walked for a couple of days to the top of the mountain. I finally decided to walk into a small town to the train station. The place was completely alien to me. It wasn't even marked on the map. I didn't know what direction to go. I had to go back to the border by myself, but I was lost. Chris had all the experience; I was the follower. I decided to try to return home. I didn't think about the possibility of the police calling my home town. I thought all the excitement was over.

When I got close to the country train station, I sat in a cornfield for a day to watch the movements. I can't remember the name of the town, if I ever learned it. The station was very small. The local passenger train stopped there. When the next train arrived at 9 p.m., four soldiers got off with a dog. They walked beside the station. I was expecting them to scan the cornfield, but they didn't. It was quite dark, because the train station had only one small electric light. As I sat there, the mosquitoes had me for dinner. The next day I crept back to the same vantage point where I had been the night before. I waited for the next train to come. When it pulled in, the passengers got off onto the platform in front of station; I was on the other side, in the cornfield. I waited for all the passengers to disembark, and then I went under the passenger cars to look for a place to crawl up into, to stow away. Before we had left home, my friend and I had studied everything under the passenger cars and the hiding places under them. My feet were to lie on one of the brake supports. The lower part of my body would rest on the other support. My shoulders were to lie on the car support. That's how we planned to cross into Yugoslavia. I travelled under the passenger car for two hours, until I got into a big city. I immediately recognized where I was and how to get home. When I arrived home the next day, I told my wife what had happened. Then I went to Chris's family and told them what had happened with Chris and how we got separated. His parents were crying and very concerned about him. I didn't know what to do.

For two weeks I waited for Chris to come home. He didn't make it. There was a place in our home town where we agreed to meet if we ever became separated. He was nowhere to be found. I knew that he had been caught. Then, after two weeks, the Romanian police arrested me at home. At the police station, they asked me how I had opened the handcuffs. I realized that I was in big trouble. That night, an officer came and took me back to where I had been caught. We travelled by train, and I was in handcuffs. When I got to the police station, he put me in the town jail. Chris was two cells down from me. He had been there all the time I was gone. The captain who had originally escorted Chris and me to the jail became so angry about our escape that he beat Chris very badly. We spent two more weeks there – a most miserable place. It was dirty and bug-infested. I was afraid to touch anything. The odours were magnificent. We had one single, open faeces/urine bucket for everyone in the cell; the bucket was emptied once each day. P U! The guards told us that that when we escaped to another country, we might get to use a toilet, but not here. I sat in that room for two weeks without washing my face, because there was no water. When I asked for a shower, the police officer told me the shower didn't work there but, when we got to prison, we would have one. Most of us had only attempted to cross the border.

After two weeks of misery, we were finally transferred to a regular prison. Twenty of us travelled on the bus. They took us to Popa Sapca Prison, which was located in Timisoara. Of course, I got to talk with Chris for a while, because they transferred both of us in the same bus. When I looked at his face, both sides were still bruised. After a month, I could see clearly where he had been beaten. I wasn't angry with him, because I knew it was my fault. I still loved and cared for him like a good friend. I asked him what had happened and how he had got caught. After a short conversation, I found out that he had been caught the very next day in the same city. After a small pause, I asked him what he had been doing in the city anyway. He gave no answer. Then I realized my mistake. I had put my trust and confidence in the wrong man. The words of my dear wife came back to me; not to listen to Chris, because he was only 19 years old – just a kid. I had neglected to heed her advice, and now I was in big trouble again. In a short time, I was back in prison. There was nothing I could do or say, because it was my fault. I was supposed to control myself, not someone else. I had another broken heart. I thought Chris might have learned something from the experience – but he gained nothing from it. The prison was in Timisoara. All of us were there for the same "crime" – searching for a better life. They all looked for a better future, just as I did. Of course, I wrote to my dear wife to tell her where I was. The prison wasn't much different from the last one. Here, nobody was taken out to work, especially since our common crime was escaping! We stayed inside 24 hours a day, every day. I can't forget the first shower

I had after two weeks. My skin itched all over. I didn't count on the water being so cold. I could only wash my head and feet. The prison was super-clean and the officers cared a lot about cleanliness. Sheets were washed once a week, and we took a shower once a week. It had a big toilet. There was a big sink where I could wash my face. It was much better than the jail we had come from. After two months, the prison officials took me to court. Sixty of us were on the bus for the same thing – attempting to cross the border and be free. I saw Chris again, and talked to him. He was much better than before (we were separated because he was under 21).

Back to the Incubator

AFTER FOUR HOURS, WE RETURNED TO the prison. Everything was moving quickly. Anyway, I was sentenced to two years in prison for attempting to cross the border illegally and for escaping. Chris was sentenced to the same thing. After I was sentenced, I ceased talking to anyone. I realized that my efforts at freedom had been indecisive and, consequently, had just cost me two more years of my life under the hammer and sickle. I finally realized that my life was going to be very short and unpleasant unless I escaped. I was moved into another room with twenty-two men. Of that number, eighteen faced the same charge: attempting to escape. I listened to all of them. I didn't talk. I learned all their mistakes – especially how they got caught. I gained lots of information from them; good, vicarious experience. We usually clustered in small groups of 4 or 5. That was mostly for our discussions. I started keeping a detailed mental catalogue of all the most dangerous situations from Romanian and Yugoslavian territories. I had to learn all that they knew, and then decide which ones were fools. I didn't want to depend on anyone any more, especially the fools. From Romania through Yugoslavia to Austria there were lethal hazards. Many men made it, but more did not. Once in Austria, you were free, but there were so many mistakes to avoid before then.

I changed my plans – I decided against a Black Sea escape. I knew that I would have more moves, and better and faster movement, through the countryside. I started to study the Yugoslavia-Romania border. I learned how the soldiers scheduled their dog patrols. I also learned which civilians to avoid. The people who lived near the borders were the most dangerous. We had to hide during the day because, if they saw us, we would be turned in to the police or the soldiers. The state had set a bounty for our capture.

The farmers made a habit of ploughing neat, wide borders around their fields so they could see our footprints. They could turn us in without even seeing us! I also learned that, at night, the Romanian soldiers shot first. There was no surrender at night – you just died at the border. No justification was required. I heard of many instances where individuals or whole groups were gunned down at night. The groups were mostly families trying to run together: wives, children, etc. They died at the border because the Romanian government viewed them as embarrassing failures and mistakes. I also met lots of men who had been severely beaten by the soldiers. Many died after a few days in captivity. I saw mutilated faces, broken jaws, ribs, hands, legs, badly-bruised bodies and dog bites. We were blood sport for the sadistic guards. They got to hurt men and abuse women and children, almost at will. It was evil. Two of my new acquaintances told of their wives being killed because they resisted the sexual abuse of the soldiers who had caught both families trying to escape at the border. Both women were shot. The men were charged and sentenced to one year and 6 months in prison. Of course, Romania did nothing; no punishment for the soldiers. Lots of bodies were left at the border, some shot, some bayoneted. I heard all these things, yet I never thought of giving up or doubting myself. My dream of escaping was still with me. I didn't think I would be shot at the border like others. I knew the next time would be different. My dream grew bigger than before. Anyway, I learned of all the risks and dangers of the Romanian border. The other problem was with the Yugoslavian people on their side of the border. They knew of every illegal person who crossed or walked to the other side and through the small towns. They called their police, and the immigrants were immediately caught, especially those not having a plan. Most refugees were caught no more than 40km from the Yugoslavian border; caught just because they walked into someone's yard to drink water, or because they asked for food. Sometimes the police were at the doors, waiting to arrest them. Most refugees didn't make it as far as the city of Zrenjanin, which was 100km from the border. More than 70% were turned back at the Romanian border. The soldiers picked them up and started beating them and asked, "Why do you come back to us?" And of course, later, they were unrecognizable. The number actually escaping was very small. The Yugoslavian immigration authority (after an interview of those who were caught) accepted only those who were persecuted by the Romanian government. My problem on my first escape attempt was that I had to make it to the city of Zrenjanin, but I didn't know what personal facts qualified someone like me for asylum in Yugoslavia. I had decided not to take that risk again. If they turned you down, they sent you back. This time, I was going to cross the River Danube and pass straight through Yugoslavia to Austria.

The Danube River Bridge was special. It was watched by police, who patrolled it constantly. The people who lived around it did, too. I didn't speak Serbian so I would never have blended in and been able to pass myself off as a local. Besides not knowing the language, I had no suitable clothes. Serbian, I was not! The Serbian police would have spotted me instantly. Even to ask anyone in Yugoslavia a question in the Romanian language would have led to arrest. I explained to all my new jailhouse friends how to travel under a train. In particular, I showed them how to hide under the train passenger cars, which had more elaborate undercarriages. Of course, I explained every detail and body position one could use to ride. I was surprised to discover that no other detainees knew of these techniques. I encouraged them and I told them that it worked.

To travel by passenger train, I had to learn the distances and times between the cities. I repeated all the small details over and over, just like in maths class. I had all the descriptions, in detail, of the small towns and cities of Yugoslavia and Romania. I also learned how I had to act under pressure. I was prepared and, in turn, I was preparing my friends. There was a wide age spectrum, and we didn't all want the same things. Most of us were married with families, who waited for us with the dream of one day being free, too.

Most of the good information I got in exchange came from the Romanian men who lived close to the Yugoslavian border. And, of course, they told us every detail they could remember. This was most important to me, who knew nothing about the border. I mentally catalogued all my journeys, place by place, for future reference. I knew I would never give up my plans to escape, even if it might mean my death.

My wife never came to visit me – she didn't have the money for the trip. She did send me cigarettes and food every month, when the prison allowed – once every 3 months. I missed all of my family, but I knew I had to stay in prison for two years. The guards had nothing to do with us, especially when someone was sick or hurt. We were treated like outcasts. There was much brutality and humiliation from the prison guards. We were like wild beasts to them, not human any more. They kept us in abject fear, constantly. I asked for an aspirin once, and the guard told me to wait until I escaped to the west – they had free aspirins. I got very tired of the negative talk about us because we wanted to leave. The guards always tried to provoke us so they could beat us. Time went slowly. I had nothing to do; no books or Bible, except the newspapers of the Communist Party and, of course, the president, Nicolae Ceausescu, his visits. We just sat all day. I was sick of that room, but there was nothing I could do. Two years later, I was released again. I couldn't believe I was free once again to smell freedom.

Try, Try Again

I HAD NO MONEY, NO CLOTHES or other provisions and I had to report to the police station when I got home. I truly didn't know where to go. I was thinking of going straight back to the border but, on the other hand, I wanted to see my dear wife and the rest of the family. I was a little hobo looking around for a familiar face. But there were no familiar faces, only familiar things: flowers, cars, stores, traffic and the bustle of urban life. Everything became momentarily new for me. I decided to go and see my dear wife, so I went back to my home town. My wife had a job just to survive. She was glad to have me home. We sat down and I told her my plans for the future. She understood and agreed with me. It was August 1987. She was heavily burdened by our debt. We owed a lot of money to her family. I was embarrassed by our debt. I really didn't want to hear. Her mum and brother helped her all the time while I was gone. They also knew my plans, because I told them everything, and they agreed with me in my decision to leave. I told them all the dangers at the borders of Romania and Yugoslavia. I told my brother-in-law, but I didn't take him with me. I told everyone that this time I'd go by myself.

The security police weren't too happy to see me back. I had to go to the police station to report to them. Of course, they asked question after question, like, "Why do you want to leave this country?" or "Where do you want to go?" I did not answer their questions, because I knew they were looking for trouble. I remember that when I walked into that city, nobody would stop to talk with me. Not even people from the church where I used to go with my wife. I truly was a "stranger" in that city! But I didn't really care. I didn't intend to look for a job, because I knew my time was very short and I would be on the road again soon. The season was the perfect time of year to leave, because the fields were loaded with vegetables and fruits. I stayed about 20 days with my wife and then I said goodbye to her once again . In September 1987, I left to go back to the border. All the information was still fresh in my mind. I didn't want to waste my time sitting around. We went to our relatives and I told them that I was leaving once again.

I left that night on the bus and then I took the train. Oh, what excitement! I travelled with the passengers for about 6 hours. Then I took a train which went close to the border with Romania, through the small towns; I travelled for about 30 minutes and then I left the train, because the soldiers boarded it for searching. I went to a tobacco shop and bought a pack of cigarettes, and then I walked through the station. I walked like I belonged in that town, because one of the soldiers was watching me. When the train left, I returned to the train station and then I crossed to a field of corn. I sat for 30 minutes, watching for movement. It was very hot. I moved a little bit deeper into the cornfield and sat down to rest. I was waiting for night. I had to respect the plan this time and make no mistakes. I had no money and no food. I had one cigarette lighter in my pocket. I travelled very light. I walked alone. It took me 5 nights to get to the border. Of course, during the daytime, I did not move at all. After 5 p.m., I'd rise up and look all around to see if I could spot any trouble. But I stayed still. That fifth night, I saw something suspicious in front of me. It was about 500 metres away. It was one of the border-guard towers, where the Romanian soldiers watched the border; I knew I would not be able to cross there. It was just before daybreak. I went back into the cornfield and sat down to rest. I was already in the kill zone for illegals. I stayed there until 2 p.m., then I went back towards the towers to get a more precise picture. I was between two towers. The soldiers stood in the towers, looking all around. I saw Yugoslavian territory. The cornfield where I stood was lush and green and very tall. I was well concealed, but not well protected: bullets would have found me easily if I was ever seen. So, I was as afraid as I had ever been in my life. I was forced to cross there, it was the only way. I knew that the guards' shift had to change at 2 p.m. At about 1 p.m. I started to crawl low down towards the border. I knew that the soldiers would leave the towers to talk with their replacements before going back to their base. At the edge of the cornfield, between me and the border, was a field of sugar beet. The plants were also lush and green but, unfortunately, they weren't very tall plants, so I was on my stomach, waiting for the shift change. I stopped at the edge of the beet field. The last 100 metres to the border were only tussocks of grass – almost no cover at all. After that was the border. I was acutely aware of everything around me. My heart was pounding like a bass drum. At about 1:30, I saw the soldier come down from the tower. My heart started beating faster and faster. I knew I had to get up and run the last 100 metres. I waited until the soldiers had walked about 600 metres. Now there was over a kilometre between me and his rifle muzzle. I was betting that he wasn't an expert shot. I knew he couldn't make it back to the tower, no matter what he did. I got up and started to run. The leaves of the beets slapped my legs loudly as I ran. He had to have heard. But I knew I was closer to the border and cover than he was to the tower. It was too late for the soldier. When he looked up, I was at the border. He left his rifle on the ground and started to chase me. I knew that if I crossed the border into Yugoslavian territory, he would be breaking the law by following me. I heard him yelling to me, "Come back," but I kept going. I didn't want to hear. I ran for an hour, non-stop. When I got into a cornfield across the border in Yugoslavia, I knew the immediate danger was over. The corn stalks in Yugoslavia were much taller than the ones in the Romanian fields I had just left, so I had to walk a long way to the top of a hill before I could see back to the guard towers I had just run between, to the Romanian fields I had just left. I was wet and scratched. It was more than 10km into Yugoslavia when I calmed down and realized my extreme thirst and hunger. And that's when Mother Nature presented me with one large, plump, delicious watermelon, growing there in the cornfield. I made short work of half of it, and then I was able to walk normally again.

It was the seventh day and it rained hard. Everything on me got wet. I had a good shower, just missing the soap, but at least it washed off the watermelon. I walked to a nearby farm and hid in the hay barn. I rested there quietly until the next morning! I was very, very tired. Unfortunately, I snore badly and that's how I got caught. The farm dog heard me snoring and began to bark at the barn. When I awakened and looked around, I realized that I had made a dire mistake. But it was too late – the owner of the barn had called the police. They waited for me to come down from the top of the barn and, when I got down, the policeman handcuffed me. He asked if I was from Romania. I told him that I was a refugee. We took off in the police car to the station, or so I thought, but he continued to drive until he got to a big city. He drove over 80km. On the outskirts of the city, I saw the name. It was Zrenjanin, which had been my intended destination. He took me to the city jail. It was a big, stone house in the city, but the iron bars on the windows gave it away. When I got there, they put me with the other Romanian men, in one big room. They gave me food and I finally got warm. Food was different from that in my country. I saw a big difference. Even though the building was stone, the floors were warm, comfortable wood, and the rooms were well-heated. This was no Romanian dog kennel. Maybe it was jail, but it was comfortable. The cafeteria-style food was very good and spicy. There, they had the best bread I had ever eaten. Yugoslavia was known for its exotic breads. The jail was no exception. The next day, they took me to the immigration authority. I told them that I wanted to go to Australia. After my interview, the police took me back to jail. I was told that the immigration authority would decide my case in 60 days. So, for the time being, I had to stay in jail. I sat in a room with all the refugees from my country. I learned that some of us would be allowed to go, but some would be returned to Romania. I knew all these things from my country, because we discussed this in the Romanian prison. Fear came over me, because I did not know whether I would be sent back. I did not know what criteria they used to decide who would stay and who would go back to Romania.

On the fourth day they took me out to work, digging some kind of canal for electricity. Nevertheless, I enjoyed the work. But then I saw the opportunity to escape! I knew I would run, because I did not trust the Yugoslavs. Two days later, I ran away from my escort by telling him I needed to use the bathroom. I was gone in no time.

I ran through fields of corn for an hour. Then I stopped in a cornfield until night. Though I was far away, I could still see a lot of police cars running back and forth on the road. I didn't move from the field of corn where I was hiding. Then, at about 10 p.m. that night I started to walk, parallel to the road but keeping about 400 metres between myself and the road. That way, I knew nobody could see me in the darkness. During the daytime, I rested. I was in no hurry. Finally, I began to see things I had learned about in the Romanian prison where I had just spent two years. I put my knowledge to good use. Everything fell into place as I had conceived it in my mind. I walked around the small towns, cities, farms, etc. I ate fruit and vegetables. They were really good and fresh. This method of eating enabled me to avoid all people.It took me 10 days to get to Belgrade. My last big obstacle was the bridge over the River Danube. This place was most dangerous. Hundreds of Romanian "rabbits" got caught at the bridge. The police patrolled constantly in cars. But it was easier for me, because I was by myself. I could get lost easily in the crowds. I hung around the bridge in the woods until I got to know all the routines of the locals and the police. Finally, I decided to cross at noon, because everything slowed down then. It was 12:00 when I stepped on to the bridge. I walked slowly but relaxed. Quickly, I was across, unnoticed. I got to Belgrade and walked to the train station. I saw the train that went to Vienna (in Austria) and I finally found its number. I knew all the tricks police use to identify immigrants. I knew all the tricks from my country, because I had learned the hard way. I was ready to move on and not to stay too long in the train station.At about 7:30 p.m. I got under the train – a passenger car – and I rode there for 10 hours until I got to Ljubjana, the last city on the border between Yugoslavia and Austria. The weather was excellent to travel in. That night it didn't rain. The air was still warm. The train wasn't going too fast but it didn't stop, either. At small cities it slowed down. Only in the big cities, it stopped for maybe 10 minutes. It wasn't too bad. The only problem was that the wheels made lots of noise. Anyway, in Ljubljana I got out and immediately walked away from the train station. It was early in the morning, so I hid in the forest. I slept on the ground until 10:00 a.m. It was cold and I started to move around to stay warm. That locale had high hill and mountains. I started to walk through the forest and began climbing a hill. That day the sun didn't come out. The humidity was high. The grass, trees and everything around me were wet. I detected no movement around me, so I travelled a little bit faster. When I got to the top of the hill, I saw the Austrian border. I was ecstatic; I saw myself truly free at last from all my troubles. I forgot all my pain, hunger and, of course, my loneliness. All I saw was my new home, of which I had dreamed for a long time.

Back to the Romanian Gulag

I SAT DOWN AND WATCHED CAREFULLY for a few hours. During this time, I saw nobody move near me. I sat there through the afternoon. About 4 p.m. I decided to walk into the forest, because it was more secure there. Just as I got into the forest, a soldier stopped me with his rifle in his hand. I was in shock. I did not know what to do. I was caught again! I tried to tell the soldier that I was a refugee from Romania. I tried to explain it by signs with my hands, but he didn't understand. They sent me back to Ljubljana Prison. After the interview, the police found out about my escape from the Zrenjanin jail. Four days later I was transferred back to the same jail from which I had already escaped. Two officers escorted me back, handcuffed. There was nothing I could do. When I got to Zrenjanin, they were waiting for me and were "hot." I was beaten very badly and, after a week, I was returned to Romania. Oh, what a dark day; what discouragement! All I could see were prison bars and nothing else.

The authorities in Yugoslavia took me to the Romanian post control and left me there. I was picked up by the soldiers and transferred to a Romanian army base. The army asked how and from where I had crossed. Of course, I told them, and they knew exactly the place because they had found my footprints at the border. A couple of days later, I was transferred back to prison. I found myself in the same prison as before. I wrote to my wife to tell her what had happened. She was glad to know that I was alive. She started to send me what I needed in prison, which she already well knew without any instruction from me. I did not want to talk with anybody because I knew all about prison. I meditated on my mistakes and what not to do next time. I did meet lots of new people wanting to leave Romania, but they had no knowledge of how to do it. I offered my advice and experience to help them so that they would not come back to prison like me. I took my time with them and I explained each piece of the journey. I explained about the borders, people from Yugoslavia, and the bridge over the River Danube and, of course, travelling under the passenger trains. All those things were new to them, just like when I heard it for the first time. I was glad to teach them, even if I spent hours doing it. My desire was that they should all succeed and not return to prison. About 3 months later, I was sentenced again to one year and 6 months. This was my second time with the same charge, but I never thought of giving up. This time, the government transferred me to different prisons. When I was sentenced, I was in Papa Sapca Prison, in the city of Timisoara. Then, one night, I was transferred with another 100 men (with the same charge) to Gherla Prison, which was up north. They scattered all of us in different rooms. This prison was maximum security. Only those who had 25-year murder charges were there, and us.

When I entered the prison I saw many different things. The prison was of old construction, with one-and-a-half-metre-thick wall. It had 3 floors. The centre of the building was a courtyard. The denizens were of various ages and there for various rule infractions. The police put us there to discourage us, but the other prisoners were good to us. Lots of men asked me why I was there. I told them what caused me to leave the country. I told them what was going on with the Romanian communist regime and the changes in the country that had taken place. But I don't believe they understood. They had been there for many years; they didn't know that changes had taken place almost overnight. We walked inside the prison. They were pleasant to us. We didn't all have to stay in a locked room. The food was the same, but more of it. The officers were different and that made all the difference in the whole prison. They didn't care why we were there, they just wanted respect. They got it. It was a good trade. Most of the officers in that part of the country had a different mentality. They understood why we wanted to leave the country. The prison was very clean. If I had any problem I could talk to any guard and it would be corrected with other people. Lots of men realized the changes in the country and they were in agreement with me. But, in a short time, I was moved to another prison.

At the new prison I received a letter from my dear wife about her mother's death. I was shocked. I didn't know what to say – I cried. I knew there was no possibility that I could go home for the funeral. One of the officers called me and told me the bad news. I thanked him and walked away. He understood the pain and he didn't say anything else.

He just told me not to blame myself. My family was collapsing. Another person from my family left this world to be with the Lord Jesus. She was a mother to me, but we never argued. Our disagreements had all been over principles, not personal provocation. All those memories came back to me, especially all the good things she had done for me. She was the last anchor in our family. She was Pentecostal all of her life. I remember when she prayed for me, especially to receive Jesus in my heart, but I ignored her many, many times, although she had the assurance that, one day, I would accept Jesus and the church. Well, it didn't happen in her lifetime.

I knew the family would be divided later on without a strong leader. I also knew that the rest of them looked to me and my wife to take Grandpa's place. But I was in prison – there was nothing I could do for them. I already had my mind made up and all of them knew that. I wasn't ready to take that place yet, if ever. Also, the Pentecostal Church expected me and my wife to come to church and bring the rest of the family, but that could not be my burden. I had to survive state security and leave Romania, and any church commitment would have meant abandoning my plans to leave.

In 1988, during the 18 months I had been sentenced to, I was trans-ferred to Bircea Prison. The prison was the same one in which I had been held for my labour union activism. There, I was close to my Aunt Victoria and her daughter and family. I didn't serve all 18 months. In the spring, many prisoners (including me) were given a general amnesty by the Romanian government. I had served only 8 months. I was free to plan my next escape!

I made the obligatory trip to visit my poor Nina. All the while I felt badly, because I had to leave without her. I knew she loved and cared about me. And she wanted to be free, just as I did. I hoped that, one day, I would get her and make our lives in a better place. She understood that, by going through all this trouble (especially prison), we might have a better life in the West rather than in a communist regime. I never intended to abandon her. I knew a man should have one wife, as my Grandpa Glava had taught me from the Bible, and she felt the same as I did. However, people told her that I was not the right man, because I wanted to leave the country. But she wanted freedom, just as I did. After my mother died, my wife was the only person I could trust and count on.

She was very sincere and she was a woman of integrity. All the time I was gone she was faithful to me. Anyway, she knew I was coming home one day.

My Life in Chaos in Lupeni

I CAME BACK FROM PRISON for the third time, without money or clothes. I went straight back to my home town. When I arrived at my apartment, I knocked on the door, but Nina didn't answer. It was 10 o'clock at night. Well, I thought she could be with her little sisters, about half mile away, so I went there and saw my wife's Aunt Margaretta. I asked, "Where is Nina?" She looked shocked and didn't know what to say. I felt something was wrong. When I insisted, her aunt said that Nina was in another city with another man – my wife had left me for another man. She had finally grown weary of being alone. I wanted to die.

I had been gone a long time. Nina had been crushed by loneliness, so she left me. I never saw her again. And she stopped coming to see her relatives, because she was ashamed. My heart was broken. I found myself alone and an outcast. I felt like everything had changed. We had been together for 9 years and now it was all over. Everything vanished. I still cannot believe she left, but I understand the power of loneliness to destroy love. And my desire to leave Romania ultimately caused the loneliness. I guess I left her before she left me, if the truth be known.

I returned to the apartment and, when I got in, half of the furniture and appliances were gone. I wasn't interested in anything any more. A few days later, I had to move from my apartment because I owed so much money, which I was unable to pay. I had no other place to live. I was without money, clothes, a wife, friends and, of course, the relatives. I walked the streets to find some place to stay. I reported to the police station to let them know that I was back. I knew they didn't want me back in the city. They knew my wife had left me. Everybody knew my situation, especially my neighbours. I heard lots of bad things about my wife when I was gone, but I didn't care any more. Most of my friends laughed at me. They told me (even the authorities), "Hey, cowboy, you still want to live in the jungle!" I said nothing to them. I walked away smiling. I never wanted them to know my heart or my pain. I wore a mask.

I never give up on anything, so I pretended everything was fine. But inside I was badly wounded. I saw many cases in prison where my friends came to tell me, "John, my wife left me!" I thought, that's another thing which you have to face. I encouraged them to look to the future for the gain they would have one day. I encouraged them never to give up, because they could start another wonderful life and things would be much better than there. And I saw so many gain strength and start to forget their past misery. But now, it had happened to me. I never thought or expected it to happen to me. I trusted her with my life. All these things pushed me to make a firm decision not to ever come back to Romania. Anyway, I met some old friends who lived in the streets. They, at least, had respect for me. They helped me. After a while, I found a place to live, without water or toilet, but it was better than the streets. It was under Chris's family house. They knew me very well. I had to steal for food to survive. Chris's mama brought plates of food many times, for which I was grateful. After she left, the plate was quickly emptied.

Sometimes, I could not steal because I was being watched in all the stores. The store managers followed me throughout the stores. I didn't tarry, because I had no money. It was the beginning of June. I could not leave then, because the vegetables and fruit along my escape route weren't ready yet. I had to wait to the end of August or September to leave, so I could have food. I searched around for a temporary job and found one; it didn't pay much, but I had to save money for my next escape. The situation was really bad. I was depressed because of the uncontrolled turmoil in my life. It was pure chaos; but the entire country was depressed, not just me. There was a curfew after 9 o'clock at night. The streets were full of police and military. They were looking for trouble – someone to arrest. I had no rights, because they wore the uniforms. But it didn't bother me any more, because my mind was on something else.

The general Romanian population was in palpable fear, constantly. Wherever I walked, I heard complaining and discouragement. Later on, going back and forth to work, I met my old friend, Chris, with whom I had made my first escape attempt. He was in bad shape, just like me, but he had his parents and a place to stay. Nobody would hire him, because he had been sentenced for attempting to cross the border. The police had an extensive file on him, just as they did on me. Our big problem was the lack of good jobs. Companies didn't hire those who had been in prison. So, that's how we lost our identity. If I had joined the Communist Party, it would have been different; then no one would have cared if I had been in prison 10 times. But I refused to accept communism.

When Chris finally got a job where I worked, the security apparatus found out and immediately tried to have us both fired. And the security police didn't like seeing us together. They were afraid we might influence others. Many of our co-workers wanted to leave, but they didn't know how to do it. I was warned by the police not to talk to anyone because, if I did, I would be sent back to prison. And I knew anything was possible. It didn't take much in communist Romania to land behind bars. That is why I had to report to them when I came back from prison. I knew their true motivation for having me report in. It was to enable them to re-jail me at the first sign of rebelliousness or bad attitude. And the police were also aware that Chris and I knew enough to inflame the younger people. So, I could not talk openly to anyone any more. Now, when friends (acquaintances, actually) questioned me about what they had to do to leave, I told them to find out for themselves. With that, I closed the conversation. Chris and his family helped me a lot with food; I had nothing to eat. Chris's family had attended church with my wife's parents and grandparents. We knew each other from church but, in time, we drifted apart. Now, I became a part of his family. One of his sisters, Magdalena (she was 18), looked after me. But I wasn't looking for another wife.

I had been released from prison in June on amnesty and, by the end of August, I was planning to leave again. In the middle of June, I met one of my old school friends, who stopped me and asked if I intended to leave again. And I said, "Of course; I have not changed my mind!" His name was Jean. A very strong Christian man, two years my junior! He was another Christian brother I could trust. I asked him if he had saved any money, and he said, "John, I'll support you; just help me to get out of this country, too, because there is no future for me here." He, like me, wanted nothing to do with the communist regime. We had gone to school together and he lived in the same block where my mother had lived. We grew up together. He had a mum like I had, and another 3 young sisters. His sisters were scattered in different cities, but Jean's mother was there with him. He had attended the Baptist Church from a very young age and was a member. He was a man I knew I could trust. For that reason, I opened myself up to him. I told him I would let him come with me. I told him when I had planned to leave and he agreed to go with me, without question. But soon, the police found out we were hanging out together. I heard that someone from his neighbourhood had reported us to the authorities. We got an emphatic invitation one afternoon to go to the police station to talk with them. They wanted to know what we were up to. I told Jean not to mention anything about our plans. I didn't dare go myself, because I knew I would be arrested, just because I was leading Jean astray. They were looking for any way to separate me from the other young people. When Jean came home from the police station, I asked him if he had told the police that we shared an apartment. He said that he didn't mention anything about our plan. I was very depressed, worried and, most of the time, angry. The time went by quickly. The police knew what I was going to do, but not when. It was time for my next escape.

I kept my menial job, even though it didn't pay well. It was still better than nothing. My supervisor liked me and respected me, and knew the situation; he would probably keep his mouth shut. He was also a man of understanding.

Two weeks before the planned escape, I went to work one day at 6 a.m. After my shift was over, my supervisor asked me if I would work overtime, 4 extra hours. I agreed to do so – I needed the extra money. About 3 o'clock that afternoon, I became ill. I felt a severe pain in my stomach. I fell to my knees but, within 10 minutes, I had regained some strength. The employees immediately gathered around me to help, but I said I was OK. But the second time I fell down, I lost consciousness. When I awakened, I was in a hospital bed. I had already had surgery for a bleeding duodenal ulcer. I asked the doctor what caused it to happen. The doctor explained that the ulcer had been caused by worry and depression. I had no more questions for him. He was right about the stress. Only the Lord God knew what was going on inside of me. When I looked at my body, I saw the incision and two tubes in my right side. The nurse told me to be careful, because the incision was fresh. I realized I would have a long recuperation. I was disappointed. I had nothing to say. The nurse told me I was a miracle, because I had survived that critical condition. The nurse was a young woman who watched me constantly. She tried to make me laugh but I didn't pay much attention. I was flat on my back looking at a ceiling. All I could think about was that my postponed freedom would be coming very soon. Of course, Jean found out I was hospitalized and he immediately came to see me. I told him not to come any more. To do so would cause the police to watch him. He understood and he went and told all Chris's family the same thing. Jean knew they cared for me. The next day, as I was recuperating at the hospital, Magdalena (Chris's sister) came to see me. I couldn't believe she had come. She asked me if everything was all right. I told her I was just happy to be alive, but that I was lonely. I asked her how things were at home, and she told me that her entire church was praying for me. I asked her to bring me something to read, and she came back the very next day with a Bible. I wondered why in the world she had brought me a Bible. I wanted to ask her for another book, but I didn't want to be rude. I knew she was a Christian, so I accepted the Bible graciously. I said nothing to offend her, and that alone made me happy. I had wanted to tell her what pain I was going through, but she knew, and that's why she brought a Bible. In that time, I remember that nearly all of my relatives and friends abandoned me. I had nobody on my side. I just couldn't believe it, especially of my best friends. I was visited by some others who I didn't expect, but Magdalena was the only one who visited me regularly. My Aunt Victoria came from another city once to see me. I explained to her what had caused my illness and the need for surgery. She asked me to come to her apartment when I got out from the hospital and to stay for a while until I got my strength back.

The surgery was healing well. After two weeks I walked out of the hospital. The doctor gave me a lot of instructions. He told me what I could eat and what not to eat. What I was allowed to eat I couldn't find. When I left the hospital, I had no place in town to go. I was discharged from the hospital at 11 o'clock and I walked to a little park with benches and flowers. I sat on one of the benches, wondering where I should go. Then, I saw Magdalena coming toward me. She asked what I was doing there. She thought I had come out for a walk and was to return to the hospital. She didn't know I had been released. She asked how my surgery went and I showed her. It looked much better day by day. She started to tell me about her church and how good a time she had the past Sunday morning. I was only thinking of where I could find a place to sleep so I ignored her, especially the conversation about her church. Then, after a little pause, she started to tell me that her parents had told her that I was welcome at her home when I got released from the hospital. They would take care of me. I was incredulous, so she repeated it again for me. I got up from the bench and said, "Let's go!" Then she understood that I had been released. We both cried and we walked slowly to her home. Jean knew about it, too, and he offered help to me. Jean also knew I had no place to go. But I could not stay with him in his apartment because of the police. They watched me constantly and they wanted to know every move that I made. Jean visited me in secret and helped me by continually giving me food, money and clothes. Sometimes I stayed surreptitiously at his apartment, but mostly at Magdalena's. That way, the police lost track of me. I walked at night only; I did not want to be seen by anyone. I was careful not to be in the wrong places.

The surgery healed but I was still in pain. I didn't let it bother me, though. For some reason, I continued reading the Bible, even after I was released from the hospital! There were a lot of spiritual things I didn't understand.

Jean's mother found out about my leaving the country. She didn't want Jean to associate with me because she knew I had been in prison three times. This made me the 'bad boy'. As a matter of fact, the whole city knew about my bad attitude. I was a running joke in more ways than one! They said to one another, "The dreamer is back." But I didn't care what they said; I knew that in September, the fields would be full of vegetables and fruit – food for rabbits like me.

The First Leg of the Escape – Dodging the Watchers

THE NIGHT WE MET TO LEAVE, the excitement was exhilarating; I felt like I could fly. We left the next afternoon on a passenger train. We travelled for 5 hours by train.

This time I had altered the plan. I did not take the same route to the border as the year before. I knew the Romanian police would notice our absence from the city, and it would be easy for them to make just one telephone call to the army base and have us intercepted; so I went the other way.

When we began our walk from our last train station we were warm and dry, so we were able to move slowly. I still could not walk fast, because of my surgery. It was three weeks since I had been laid open. I could not walk too long because I didn't want to risk damaging the incision.

When we left the train, we started walking toward the border for the third time. I had no fear, but discretion demanded that we walk only at night. During the day we would hide and rest. The only problem we had was the mosquitoes – they tried to suck us dry whenever we stopped. We never left the fields of corn, unless it was night. During the day, we sat quietly among the corn stalks. Occasionally, I looked around for objects I might recognize. We took very little food with us, because I had told Jean we could not rely on food we carried – it would give us away as travellers and slow us down.

Anyhow, we neared the border on the fourth day. That last night we walked a little longer than we should have and in the morning, as we got to close to the border, we had to stop immediately because the daylight came. We quickly found a good hiding-place. In the afternoon I looked around and saw the tower on my left; it was about 500 metres from us. I began to shake because I was so close to it. We were already in the most dangerous zone. If the soldiers searched, we would be caught again.

It was about 4 p.m. and it was hot. The sky was clear.

At 11 o'clock that night we started to crawl on our bellies. I was in front; Jean followed. We couldn't stand up because we would be seen and shot immediately. We dragged ourselves on the dry ground for 4 hours and, finally, we crossed the border where the ground was ploughed. We had made it to the other side! I was so happy, but still very quiet, when I rose and began to walk normally. Jean didn't realize we had crossed to the other side – his eyes were constantly fastened on me and every move I made. He watched only me. That way, he kept his courage and was not frightened. He did what I did and stayed calm. He was inexperienced, so I had to bolster his confidence. I learned all these things in Romanian prison. Anyway, I began to laugh and he became confused. Then I sat down and, in a low voice, I told him that I wasn't laughing in mirth, but that I was laughing for joy, because we were out of Romania. We were free.

The Second Leg of the Escape – Roughing it in Yugoslavia

AFTER AN HOUR OF WALKING in Yugoslavia, we stopped to rest. I had pushed too much that night. I was ecstatic, but I was still worried about my weak surgical scar, because it might rip loose and I would be stuck there, bleeding slowly to death. If I was caught for the second time in Yugoslavia, I would be immediately sent back to Romania. So, I had to make no mistakes. That night, we walked continuously but slowly. As day broke, we looked behind us and saw the border far away.

We stopped and rested in a big field of tall, green corn. Even in the small things, I could immediately tell that this land was different from Romania. The vegetables were luscious and the plants were altogether richer and healthier than those in Romania. We rested all day. I knew the dangers weren't over – the people from Yugoslavia in that border locality were very dangerous, and all it would have taken was to be seen by one person and we would have been caught. It was stiflingly hot weather. No breeze blew through the cornfield where we roasted all day, but we happily endured the salty sweat in our eyes.

When night came, we were on the move again. We waited until 1 a.m. – leaving time for the air to cool and the locals to give up for the day. This danger zone at the border was a band about 40 kilometres wide – a fast hike of about one or two days.

Beyond that, the Yugoslavians would be oblivious. No rewards were offered beyond that 40-kilometre border, so you were safe after making it that far. However, we still had to travel slowly because of my surgery.

On the fourth day, we ran out of food. That morning, we found ourselves in another small country town. We tried to push through silently but, because of the dogs and fences in front of us, we didn't make it. I could not jump the fences because of my surgery. The houses were about 300 or 400 metres apart. We were forced to stop because of the daylight. It was about 5:30 a.m. and the sun was about one spear high. We got down in a very small creek-bed. We hid in wild weeds and stayed there all day.

As I looked around at about 7 a.m., I came to realize that we were in the back yard of someone's house. The house was 300 metres from us. I told Jean that we were in danger, but we stayed and were quiet. There were dogs and farm animals inside a fence close to the house, and the last thing we needed was a barking dog. So, we ate fallen fruit and stayed down in the creek bed. I was reasonably sure the people had gone to work in their fields and that nobody was at home, but still we could not risk approaching any house. We were close to a big, green field of trees, full of very delicious apples, pears and plums, so there was no reason to move, because our breakfast was right there with us.

In the afternoon, we heard voices around the house. When I looked, I saw a man and children moving around, doing their chores with the animals. When we heard the voices, we froze. I fell back asleep but my friend kept watch. The next cornfield on the right was about two kilometres from us. It was too far to run to, so we waited. By around 9:30 p.m. it was dark again. We were ready to creep out of the weeds like rats and continue our journey.

Our next obstacle was the big road ahead, that had a lot of traffic. This international road ran from Romania to Belgrade, Yugoslavia. We planned to follow this road to the city of Zrenjanin, where I had been detained and sent back to Romania on my last escape attempt. That morning, around 3 a.m., we crested a big hill and saw a multitude of car lights in different colours. I knew I was in Zrenjanin. The dangers of the border zone were over. I recognized a few places and now it was much easier for me, because I was familiar with the city. We found a communal well and washed our faces and clothes. We sat under the big trees and rested. Nobody noticed us.

That same night we started to walk toward Belgrade. It was easier now, because we walked with the big international road to our left (south of us), several hundred metres away. Day and night, we could see the traffic or see the headlights, yet not be seen ourselves. We finally relaxed.

We were not in a hurry. We crossed fields, passed through small towns, over creeks and into forests until we got to the River Danube.

For ten days we had travelled, from the Romanian border to Belgrade. When we arrived, we could see the main Danube Bridge from a distance: it was about 600 metres long (about 2000 feet), about 12 metres wide and about 30 metres high. The bridge was iron and concrete and connected to the road we had come along. Beyond the bridge was Belgrade, our immediate objective. For us, there was no other access to Belgrade. The water was wide and deep, and the bridge was always being watched. Yugoslavian policemen constantly patrolled it. They watched your every move. Because of this, the area was very, very dangerous for us, especially given that we were strangers in that country. The next nearest bridge was many kilometres away. If we had walked to another bridge, we would have got lost.

Also, there were many houses around the bridge, and the people who lived there knew each other well. That was another danger for us. We could have been identified easily because we were strangers.

We still had to cross a long, open expanse to get to the bridge. Under the bridge were all kinds of boats. Some were fishing-boats. Jean and I watched from a distance.

We noted all of the movement around us. There were lots of people, especially children, around the water having fun – some of them swimming or playing ball. We hid in the bushes above the riverbank. We were quiet and still all day. The distance from where we sat to the bridge was about 300 metres. We were on a little hill and had a panoramic view of the river. As we sat hidden, we began to feel it might be impossible to cross to the other side before so many eyes.

Fortunately, the weather was beautiful. The day passed very slowly and we had to sit very quietly. I meditated on our next move.

We could clearly hear the conversations at the bridge. We just didn't know the language. That was frustrating, because we knew this was our most dangerous moment. Anything could happen at the bridge. There were a lot of fishermen – too many. If they had seen us, they would have immediately called the police. The problem was that fishermen were on the bridge as well as under and around it. They constantly shifted position, and any suspicious activity by us would have been quickly noticed. I had a lot of information about this bridge from Romanian prisoners. I knew how I had to operate when I got there, but I felt inadequate as I confronted the reality of the risks. However, it was different this time, because I wasn't by myself. I realized it was going to be harder than I thought.

Many of my Romanian associates had been caught at this very location, so they all had useful tales to tell. I learned all their tricks. I also learned that many men had died there. Some died when they had to jump into the water from the top of the bridge. If they were caught alive, they were immediately returned to Romania. Every one of my friends from prison talked about that bridge. The dangers there were much more than even they had perceived. After being caught or killed, no investigation was done because no one cared. To the authorities, the victims were just more dead Romanian "wetbacks." No mercy was shown at that bridge.

The first night we saw locals walking across the bridge until 11:30. After midnight, only cars drove occasionally back and forth. On the second day, we watched again. Things generally took the same course as the day before. We did not rush, but sat there and waited for the evening and for the locals to go home. At about 8 o'clock they started to move on. Some of them walked across the bridge to the other side, to Belgrade. At about 9 o'clock, the fishermen left. Everyone was slowly disappearing. The police cars were very rare.

That was the second night of the same activity, so I told my friend that this was the night we had to move. He had no idea how dangerous it was, but I didn't want to tell him because I did not want to discourage him. He never questioned me about what would be next. He was a quiet follower. Once I was clear of my bushy hideout, fear finally came over me. I looked around and people still walked around. I pretended I belonged with them. My eyes flashed left and right. After I had walked about 20 metres, Jean emerged and slowly began to follow me. He was acting like he didn't know me. I walked along the roads smoking my cigarette, trying to pay attention to everything around me. We walked slowly, very calmly, so as not to draw attention and suspicion to ourselves. Finally, Jean came close to me and we finished our stroll to freedom together. We walked together, smiling and laughing like we were carefree.

Once I had put the first foot on that bridge, I thought it was over but, after 150 metres, when the bridge was pretty high, I saw a police car approaching from behind us. I almost lost control. All I can remember is that I waved to the police car – a friendly greeting. That sign was one of the old traditions from Europe. He saluted us back and drove right on by. When I saw he was passing us, my breath came back to me. We kept on.

We had walked another 400 metres when a second police car approached us from the other direction. The driver did not even look at us, or so we thought – but who knows? He zipped right on by. It was about 10:30 p.m. when we had mounted the bridge.

After 35 minutes, we were on the other side of the River Danube. With the exception of the two police cars, all I could think about as I crossed the bridge was how much I detested Romanian prison and how the Lord God was with us. It was past 11 o'clock that night, and everything was going smoothly.

Our next objective to reach was the train station in Belgrade. The distance was relatively short, as the crow flies, but we couldn't walk directly there. This was part of my prison training – not to go the short routes or use front doors. Both are dangerous.

The Third Leg of the Escape – Riding the Brakes

WE TOOK OVER AN HOUR to get to the train station. From the bridge we meandered through the city, dodging police and dense pockets of people. As a side benefit, I got to see the wonderful lights and colourful shops. We took long looks into different shops, especially the ones with food. Dear God, were we hungry! The shops had their wares exhibited in the windows – different kinds of meats, salami and fresh or smoked sausages. The big, round cheeses, probably 30-40 pounds each, were stacked and decorated with some kind of green leaves. At the bread stores, my favourite, we got to see all kinds of artistic designs. We were exhausted and hungry, but we had to continue our walk.

We saw a big difference, especially on people's faces; smiling, laughing and carefree faces. I cried. I asked myself why Romania didn't have those beautiful shops full of food. But I already knew the answer. Jean kept saying, "Look at this shop, John!" I told him that where we were going now would be much bigger and more beautiful – I had tears in my eyes. I didn't have all the answers for my dear friend, but I was trying to comfort and reassure him. I decided not to stop and look any more, but to just keep walking. I felt like I was in another world, and I was. I was mentally thousands of miles away, trying to imagine something I had never seen before. I looked at Jean's face and I could see the joy he took in the new, small things.

The roads weren't wide, and cars were parked bumper-to-bumper on both sides. I didn't realize there were so many brands of cars. It was the first time for both of us to see such dense traffic. Many of the brand names we had never heard of before. There were many exotic colours and designs. We couldn't stop to look longer, because someone might think we were planning to steal something. The traffic moved slowly. The people didn't pay attention to us because we blended in well.

When we arrived at the train station, I searched for the track number and train number to Austria. The train station was as dangerous as the streets, just more chaotic. But we went to an area of the station away from the main terminal building. The place where we went was a service and cleaning area for all passenger cars. We hid in one of the cars and watched the main terminal. After a while, we lay down on the padded benches in one of the compartments and slept. Both of us were really tired, not because of walking, but due to the stress of our intense vigilance for potential dangers. Every small thing could cause problems for us.

I awoke at about 10:00 a.m. the next day, because the sun was being reflected into my face. Jean was already up, watching for both of us. My preconceptions didn't line up with what I saw around me, but I accepted it. We started to observe and discuss things more carefully. We saw policemen walking very aggressively. We watched all day long to see all the moves and rhythms of the terminal. We saw people being arrested, but we didn't know why. We saw lots of strange things that day. We knew we couldn't delay for another day. That place was serious trouble! Yes, there were lots of people in the station but, also, the policemen were everywhere as well. On every corner there were two or three policemen asking for identification.

I didn't waste any more time. I instructed Jean on how to stay under the train carriage. The passenger car had 4 wheels and two axles. We were to be contorted – tucked up under it. To stay secure and hidden there, we had to place both feet on the first brake-support arm and place our lower backs on the second brake-support arm. Our shoulders would lie on the frame of the car, with an axle below our feet. The axles rotated with the wheels, so we had to stay suspended between the moving axles and the passenger-car body. It was really quite dangerous and frightening, but there was no other way.

I had come up with something new that nobody suspected could be done. It looked impossible, even to my friends in the Romanian prison but, after a good explanation, some of them understood. Many of my friends said they would never try my "train ride", because the risks were too great. They searched for other solutions. Anyway, I showed Jean how to do it. Jean trusted me and, to my surprise, he had no questions. Whatever I was going to do, he was willing to follow my lead. From my explanations and prior escape attempts, he knew that the real risks were not under the train, but avoiding nosey locals and the police. The real problems were before or after the train ride. The train ride itself posed only one, simple problem – it was instant death if you fell.

Anyhow, we checked out the service area and the main terminal, looking all around for possible dangers. Because the whole station was crowded, we had the opportunity to retreat to a less crowded place where we could sit and talk. We needed to go over our plan to assess the dangers.

At around 6 p.m., we went back to our track and stood there with the passengers who were waiting for the train to Austria to depart. Jean and I didn't talk to each other. As a matter of fact, we acted as if we didn't know each other. It took about 10 minutes to load the passenger cars once the train had pushed them to the terminal. We were in the middle of the whole train line, so we had to move quickly towards the train because my plan was to hide under the second passenger car. We stopped at the second passenger car. Nobody was around us at that moment. I told Jean that I would get over the first wheel and he could get over the second. We had to go to the other side of the car to do this so we wouldn't be noticed. We walked up between the cars. As the rest of the people walked into the passenger cars, we got down on the other side between the fence and the train. We closed the door behind us. We moved quickly before someone in authority saw us. Then we crawled up under the passenger car and braced ourselves. Now it was either do or die. There is a virtue in such simplicity: it becomes easy to focus on the task at hand.

In a very short time, the train started to move, then pick up speed. In 30 minutes, the train had accelerated to 120 kilometres per hour. The sleepers beneath us blurred with speed. All I saw were the two rails and the spinning wheels. The weather was beautiful when we started but, after two hours, the weather changed and got very cold. When we got up into the mountains, the cold wind sliced through our clothes. It was terrible. We couldn't move because of the speed of the train. My position was very uncomfortable and I couldn't change it because of the spinning wheels. Now I was freezing, too. The situation was agonizing. The train was an express train, so it didn't stop often. I knew the next stop was

Zagreb, which was a 5-hour journey. When the train got to a little country station it slowed to about 70 kilometres per hour, but it did not stop. After the city limit was passed, the train picked up speed again to about 120 kilometres per hour. We passed lots of fields and bridges.

It got dark and started raining very hard around 8:30 p.m. The situation was much more difficult than I had anticipated. Our clothes were soaked. We had no extra clothes, because we had wanted to travel light and inconspicuously. We were stuck under the carriage. There was nothing we could do but brace ourselves there and get down at the first stop. Sometimes, I called to Jean to see if he was all right. I was concerned about him because the physical stress was so harsh. I could read his face, but he never said a word to me.

We arrived in Zagreb at around 11:00 p.m. We had to get down quickly, because the passengers gathered waiting for the train might see us. I had to extract my legs with both hands, because I was stuck. I couldn't move at first, because I was so cold. We had frozen and suffered for 5 hours. Jean came and pulled me out on the side of the train. When I came out from under the passenger car's carriage, I started to move quickly.

We left the train station and stopped briefly in a cornfield. From there, we walked for about 30 minutes until we came to a deserted auto junkyard. We began to rummage in the wrecked cars for clothes. Eventually, we found some rags so we could warm up and rest there overnight. Hypothermic, I shook badly for a long time. Finally, I warmed up enough to sleep.

At around 7:00 a.m. the next day, Jean woke me up and asked if I was all right. I told him that it was a miracle to be alive and that I was glad we could continue our journey. It was daylight, but the sky was dark and full of heavy clouds. As the fear and excitement of the preceding day died down, I realized that we had to travel for another 5 hours to get to Austria. We still had another two borders before us to cross. The journey wasn't over yet.

When we were not in the big city, we weren't as concerned about the local people around us. Out of Zagreb and into the countryside, the people were more understanding. My clothes dried on me. We walked around in the junkyard and finally found a well and washed ourselves.

After that we searched for food. We couldn't enter gardens with vegetables or fruit because everything was private and had fences and, of course, if we came close to a house the dogs would bark. I thought about going into a grocery store but, because of my clothes and face, I felt I would be conspicuous. As I approached one store, I saw one of the employees watching me a little too closely. I walked on. I got nothing to eat. The employees followed me until I left the area. We walked around the streets and, finally, we did find some discarded bread in a trash can. We ate it in no time. Then we saw other people in the streets just like us, except they were Yugoslavian and spoke the language. We saw a lot of small shops with beautiful designs and ornaments around them. We looked from a distance because we didn't want to be followed again as if we were gypsies, so we just nodded and walked.

The city was very dirty and very loud. Many small cars flew up and down the roads. The people in the street appeared very friendly and hospitable, but we could not communicate with them. When two or three people met together, they hugged. I realized it was their tradition. We saw crowds everywhere and lots of street markets. The sweet smell of sausages, fish and chicken permeated the air. The squares were jammed with farmers selling their merchandise. It was happily noisy. The people wore the traditional, colourful clothes of the countryside. Most of the city was old buildings, interspersed with tiny parks with benches and flowers. It was afternoon, and we spent our time walking around with nothing to do. We should have been resting, but we were hungry and curious.

Later on, we went back to the train station in Zagreb. We waited, hidden in a nearby cornfield all afternoon. The weather was still threatening, but we refused to waste time thinking about the consequences of failure. We expected another rainy night, but we had to continue. It was easier to continue than to go back. The rain was rough, but it also concealed us and helped us to move quickly. I knew also, from my experience, that the rain would keep the police inside. The bad weather considerably lowered our risk of detection. I also knew the Yugoslavian patrols would not spend their time walking around the train station and checking under the carriages in the rain.

The risks of a foot-crossing are too great, because two days in the 40-kilometre zone are too much. Both the police and the border denizens provide too many eyes. Trains are really the safest way to go, provided you can hang on in the wet and cold. I knew the border patrols would check the passengers at Ljubjana – more information from the Romanian prison. We had to travel for another 3 hours from Zagreb to Ljubjana. We knew another bone-chilling ordeal was waiting for us. It was raining, so we covered ourselves with clear plastic to protect ourselves from getting wet. We were still in the cornfield.

Night fell and, at about 10:30 p.m., we re-entered the main terminal and waited for our train to come. It was the same express train we had ridden the night before – the one to Vienna. As we waited for the train, we kept calmly active so as not to draw suspicion to ourselves. The passengers here didn't care about us – only the police did. Because of this, we didn't come too close to the policemen, soldiers, or curious civilians. When the train arrived, it would be there for only 15 minutes. As it pulled in, I noticed that the passenger cars were wet and muddy. I knew we had to ride on those cold, wet and muddy wheels and brake-boxes, no matter how uncomfortable and cold. This time, we waited until the last possible minute to get under the carriage. Just as the train started to move, we quickly got under the carriage and then on top of the brake-support arms. When the train left the covered terminal, the rain poured down on us as we got settled. We again faced a cold, wet, windy ride, made worse by the speed of the train. However, we couldn't wait for another day. The time passed agonizingly slowly. I had to stay focused on my body position. All of the metal I touched was very slippery and wet. I had to be very careful, because one wrong movement and the wheels and rail bed would reduce me to a mass of splintered bones and bloody pulp.

It was raining hard as the train approached Ljubjana. That leg of the journey took us 3 hours. The train was stopped there for about 20 minutes. Lots of passengers got off and many were waiting to get on. Although it was crowded, the passengers moved quickly. Suddenly I saw the Yugoslavian police walking around the train. It was too late to get down from under the carriage. I was gripped with fear. I thought to myself, "It doesn't matter what it takes, I will not move." Nobody had the slightest inkling that we were under the carriage. It was just too dangerous to get down, especially in that kind of weather. We were not in a hurry, except for our extreme physical discomfort. My friend asked me if we could get down and I said we could not. I knew that from this train station to Austrian territory was only another hour. I decided to stay there and be done with Yugoslavia. The rain was working for us, so we would stay put and push to the mark. I answered back to him by saying that we would get down in Austria, and he became silent. My last look at Yugoslavia was of a wet and grimy rail bed while I was freezing in agony. Yugoslavia never looked better.

Finally, after 20 minutes, the train started to move again. Thank God, we were rolling again. Once again, we picked up speed in no time as I breathed in relief. But something very curious happened after about 30 minutes of travelling toward the border. The train stopped at a very small country train station. I didn't know why, or what was afoot. That stop was totally unexpected. It was a small "whistle-stop" size train station, with only one big light in front. When I looked up, my heart stopped – I saw soldiers with dogs! I knew the Yugoslavian police didn't usually bring their dogs to the trains, and it was raining too hard for that. Then other policemen and soldiers got down from the train and started running to the station, and I realized that the soldiers at the station had only come to pick up the soldiers who had been riding on the train, checking the passengers' papers. Now they were finished. I heard the voices of the police talking among themselves. I did not know what was said, because we didn't understand Serbian. Five minutes later the train started moving again. More relief for me! Oh, what a joy – the victory was at hand. I knew our journey was almost at its end. I could almost taste freedom!

At the first stop in Austria, the Austrian police got on the train, but we were unconcerned. I knew they would help us to go on. I told Jean it was all over. He got scared and asked what I meant. I said that our journey was all over, because we were in the territory of Austria. I had so many bad memories from Yugoslavia, but now it was all over. We crawled out from under the train and walked in with the legitimate passengers. When we got inside the train station, we felt the warm air immediately. It was a changing world for both of us.

Our Austrian Debut

OUR CLOTHES WERE SOAKED. Our faces were completely blackened because of the dirty water splattered on us under the train. When I saw Jean's face, I started to laugh. He started to laugh at me – we both looked like coal-miners. We went to a bathroom to wash our faces, and we had to really soak our skin to get the soot and grime off. We looked at ourselves in the bathroom mirror and couldn't believe we were so dirty. That was when the conductor came up to us and tried to talk to us. Then he immediately backed off. Jean and I could read the fear on his face. We didn't act aggressively. We sat calmly. Neither of us understood German, so we didn't respond to his questions. Immediately, he left and returned with more train officers. They began to interrogate us, but we did not understand a single word that was said.

That morning, the conductors took us to an Austrian police station. We were not physically restrained. One of the police officers was very amiable and offered us two chairs. We sat. I couldn't believe the civility of the policeman. It was new for both of us. We were in a big room that was about 7 metres long by 5 metres wide. They were working at 4 little desks and a computer. It was very quiet in there except for the occasional ring of the telephone. The room was decorated with flowers on the desks. There was a large oriental rug in the middle of the room.

The policemen examined us and shook their heads as they discussed us. I didn't know if it was because of how we looked or what we had done. After a few minutes, one of the policemen went into another small room and came back. He handed each of us a small cup. The cups contained a sweet, brown powder we had never seen before. After adding hot water to it, we drank it. It was hot chocolate. That was the first time I ever drank hot chocolate. We were asked if we spoke German, and we shook our heads "no." The policeman asked if we spoke English. Jean knew very, very little.

Then the police got a map and asked us how we had got there. All the conversation was through hand signs and pointing to the map. We told him everything. First, I showed him Romania and the city of Lupeni, where we came from. Then I showed him the Yugoslavian territory, with the cities we had gone through. I told him that we crossed into Austria by train. I showed him our entire route and all the descriptions. His attitude was very calm and attentive. Then he asked if we had shot or killed someone in our country. We told him that Romania didn't allow private guns and we had not killed anybody. We ran from Romania only to be free. They understood where we wanted to go. All the Austrian policemen were very friendly.

Finally, one of the policemen came into the room where we were and brought us some papers. Then he made a sign to follow him. He took us in a police car to the refugee camp at Transkirchen. It was a two-hour drive. When we passed Vienna, I saw the sign and the name of the city, Transkirchen. Immediately, I recognized the name because I had heard about this city. The policeman tried to talk with us but it was no use; our language skills just weren't up to the task. But the drive was enjoyable. The countryside and small towns were beautiful and the flawless, paved country roads were like nothing I had ever seen before. I wanted to compliment the policeman on his beautiful country but he could read it on my face. He gave me a few cigarettes and I nodded in appreciation. He was a kind man who was obviously enjoying our wide-eyed awe. Our trip to cross all of Yugoslavia had taken 21 days. Now we were free! No more communist regime. I felt such peace in my heart.

Sitting in the police car, I couldn't believe it was all over. I cried. At times, my old bad memories came back to mind – prison, and losing my mother, wife, relatives, friends... and country. These memories broke my heart once again. I felt bad, especially when I thought about these things. It had all occurred so quickly and unexpectedly, but I knew I had reached my first goal. I looked at my friend. He, too, was happy and excited at everything he saw, but he didn't know what was in my heart. I responded to his excitement but, in my mind, I was already far away in the future. This time we had made it, and Jean wouldn't have to see a Romanian prison. It was like a dream for me. Even the officer was carefree and happy. You could see it in his face and smile. He was observant, but not vigilant, and he was sincerely happy to welcome us to his country. When we saw some big buildings, he slowed down the car for us to see better, explaining what the buildings were. We couldn't understand all of his explanations, but we saw many new things. I had never before seen an autobahn with 6 lanes each way. The police station was quite different from the one in my home town, and so were the people. It was very hard for me to understand, but I accepted it. He shook his head saying, "Romania, Romania; it's no good." It hurt me to hear these words about my country, but I knew he was right. I had to agree with him. Anyway, we became friends and I truly had lots of respect for him.

When he passed Vienna, he drove on for another 40 minutes to the small town of Transkirchen. At the gate of the refugee camp, the officer handed some papers to the gatekeeper. I realized that this was to be our new, temporary home. What a happy and exciting day. The Vienna policeman told us to wait at the camp gate. He returned to his car and drove away. Surely the Lord was with us.

When we got to the gate, we presented our identification and waited for our papers to be processed. We were not alone. There was a big crowd at the gate, waiting for admission to the camp. A small building at the gate was where all the entry and exit paperwork was handled. The camp was surrounded by a rough, iron fence. It was hand-made and had an ornate design. It stood about 5 feet high and was painted green. Sitting at the gate, we saw that inside to the left was a very big building. It had two floors. The camp central courtyard was very large. On the right were several more, small, buildings.

After an hour of waiting at the gate, a man came and called Jean and me inside the camp. We followed him, and were taken to the largest building and shown where our beds were. The upper floor where we were to stay was an open dormitory. It had about 20 beds per room. But, in addition, beds were all over the buildings, even in the halls: metal beds with cotton mattresses. Each one had two brown blankets, sheets, and a pillow. The communal cafeteria took the whole first floor. The food there was very good. They fed us 3 times a day. Our caretakers were very friendly. There were people from all over the world, including Russia, Poland, Yugoslavia, Turkey, China, Africa, and many, many other countries. There were many languages, many age groups, many strange cultures, and lots of little children and little babies all mixed together at this camp. The children received very special treatment and special food. Some of the people arrived well-clothed and with good travel documents. Others, like Jean and me, arrived with nothing but the clothes on our backs. All of us were looking for something better. We all had the same dreams and plans in our hearts. Everyone had his own reason to leave his home country.

Anyway, after our first supper, I took a good, hot shower and went to bed. The scar on my belly was still looking good, but this time I had a serious problem with my feet. Once I lay in my bed, I was asleep in no time. I was very tired because, in the last 24 hours, we had pushed hard to complete our escape quickly. We knew we could rest later. What joy and happiness we felt – this was our first night sleeping in a free land. No more communism or arbitrary rules over us. We had no concerns until the next day. The caretaker who showed us our beds told us that, the next day, we would have to present ourselves to the immigration office at the camp. For once we felt that government officials would act in our interests.

We awakened early. After breakfast, we went to the immigration office. There were many people ahead of us with the same purpose. Jean and I were the only Romanians being processed that morning. As I waited in front of the offices, I saw the other camp buildings separately. The camp was clean and tidy. I learned that there was an area for married people. In front of the dormitories was another separate building, containing the camp offices. The camp also had a large infirmary, located in an old and very beautiful stone-and-brick building with two floors. It was about 100 metres from my dorm. The distance from gate to our dormitory entrance was about 200 metres. In the middle of the camp was a big artesian fountain. Flowers were everywhere! All the footpaths were lined with flowers, and all the buildings were a matching cream-yellow colour.

My Transkirchen
Debriefing

IT WAS A BEAUTIFUL DAY at the beginning of October. Jean and I sat in front of the offices on benches, waiting our turn for immigration processing at Transkirchen. I wasn't worried or concerned any more, because I knew things would improve from then on. Our immigration interview was in German, but we had an interpreter who also spoke Romanian. The little Austrian official gave us two chairs and we sat in front of his desk. A slim and tall young man came from another room. He also sat. He was our interpreter. We heard the questions twice – first in German, then the Romanian. It was our first German lesson. This was more serious than school, but much more exciting. We knew that we would be helpless unless we learned our new language quickly.

The man asked our names and where we came from, and we told him. My interviewer took careful notes. He asked me to tell him why I had left my home country. I gave him a brief personal history and told him all the reasons why I had left, including my low opinion of communism.

I told him I was born and raised in Romania by my mother. I didn't have a happy life. My mum worked hard all her life to provide for both of us. It was a harsh environment, especially with only one income. We lacked necessities, and we weren't the only ones. Then the communist government changed overnight – President Ceausescu became a dictator. I was forced to learn and to submit to the communist regime while I was going to school in the army. I could not adapt myself to become a good communist patriot. I refused to become a part of the communist family. I didn't want to change my character and to let them transform me into a beast. I had intended to leave the country from a young age, but postponed leaving because my mother got sick.

I explained to my interviewer that, at the age of 18, I was quite poor. I lacked the necessities of a good life – education, food, employment and so on. Then, at 19, I compounded my problems by marrying a young girl and then taking a deadly and dangerous job as a coal-miner. I explained to the man who interviewed me that it was a short leap from the coalmine to participating in a mine labour strike, and that my labour movement activities in Romania had marked me for life. After a prison term for strike activity, I was unemployable. I really could not afford to live the good life with my wife any more, because of the high expenses. Then I promised her that, one day, I would leave the country and find a place with better conditions and opportunities. She understood my wishes and agreed to my plan. I couldn't leave at that time, because my mother was in a critical condition. I didn't want her to die knowing I had left for the West. I stood beside her and worked hard in the coalmine.

In the summer of 1977, the miners went on strike. It was no small thing, because this strike affected the whole country. At that time, I was in my second year as a miner. The strike was held for 3 nights and 3 days, and the number of strikers was over 80,000. I was a part of that. I had tried to speak up for my rights. All of the striking miners were of the lowest economic class, so the strike alarmed and frightened the communist government – an uprising of the proletariat. There was no way to punish this bottom rung of society further, short of jail or death. President Ceausescu met with the strikers at their demand. He had no choice. He had avoided it for 3 days but, as the crowds grew bigger, he knew they had to be placated, even if only with lies and false promises. When he left, nothing changed. As a matter of fact, things grew worse than before.

Then the government witch-hunt began for the strike leaders. There were many late-night arrests, killings and beatings by the security police. Many workers went into hiding. For strikers, it was dangerous to sleep at home. Many whole families just disappeared. Eventually, the authorities learned that I had been a strike participant. I told them that I had simply tried to defend my rights. I soon realized I didn't have rights any more in that country. I had struck for better wages and a better life. After interviewing me, the Communist Party knew I was totally against them. After that interview, I was a marked man in the eyes of the government.

Several years later, I was inducted into the army. I had nothing but trouble with my military superiors. The commander of my platoon realized that I totally rejected the standard military indoctrination required by the government. Because of my rejection of communist indoctrination I was, once again, branded by the communist regime as a trouble-maker. The label stuck until I left Romania.

Out of the army and back home, I got another mining job but, once again, I found myself on the periphery of labour unrest. In 1982, some of my mining co-workers became inflamed over new labour inequities. They wanted another strike to secure and solidify the 6-hour underground shift length that the government had instituted after the 1977 strike. An 8-hour shift is too long to work hundreds of feet below ground. Fatigue takes over, and miners have accidents. For that reason, my co-workers asked me to be their leader. I refused, but the mere fact that I had been asked marked me as a potential strike leader and, therefore, I was an enemy of the government.

I left without saying anything to my friends. On the second day, the police arrested me and put me in prison. I was charged with "investigation." I got sentenced at night and found myself behind bars for 6 months. One of my co-worker friends got arrested at the same time. He was also jailed on the same charge. After release, I was absolutely unemployable. None of the companies in that region could hire me.

This was the explanation I gave to my Austrian immigration investigator. I told him I was not able to find a job in other cities due to government harassment, because I had resisted the communist regime's authority. I then told him that I didn't have the money for a legal passport and, even if I had had the money, I still could not have left Romania because I had an arrest record. I had no alternative; I had to move illegally. Then I paused for a while.

The Austrian immigration officer asked me how many attempted crossings I had made. I explained that this was my third attempt. I told him that I had been caught one time in Romania and put in prison. After that I sat for a few weeks, then I ran back to the border. The second time the Yugoslavian authorities sent me back to Romania. The third time was successful. It took me about 3 years in prison to learn the tricks. Then I told him all the things that had happened on our journey from Romania to Austria. I told him how we travelled under the train's passenger cars to Austria. He shook his head in amazement. He wrote all these things down.

Then he asked if I was a Christian. I told him I went to church and people knew me there. He put his pen down and looked into my eyes. Then I said that I read the Bible and that I had one in my language. Then I realized he wanted a deeper answer. I stopped and I thought about what he wanted to know. The officer turned to Jean and asked if he was a Christian. Jean said, "Yes, sir, I was saved when I was 10 years old." The man started to smile and was obviously satisfied with Jean's answer.

I wondered to myself what being saved meant. Nobody had ever had told me these things. Many people had told me about Jesus Christ and his beautiful stories, but they were just interesting stories to me. There were lots of things I didn't understand and, for that reason, I didn't really believe. The man asked Jean how he got to Austria. Jean said he had faith in me and did what I had told him. He hadn't worried like I had. He just trusted my experience. The immigration man wrote a few more lines and then stopped. He told Jean that there were many Baptist churches in Vienna, including a Romanian Baptist Church. After that, they started to talk about the Bible for a little while. Jean told the immigration officer I was new to Christianity. It took about an hour for this whole process.

My First Coca Cola

THE TOPIC OF THE INTERVIEW turned to my health problems. My feet were swollen, battered, cut and infected. I took off my shoes and peeled down my smelly, pus-soaked socks and showed them to the officer. He got up and looked at my feet. Then he asked me about my injuries. My feet were bloody and bruised because I had gone barefoot in the fields. My feet were so bad that I couldn't get my shoes back on. He picked up the telephone and summoned two nurses. They arrived about 10 minutes later. At first, I didn't pay attention to them because I thought they had come for someone else, but they had come to care for me.

I was taken to the emergency room. They had to soak my feet so that my bloody socks could come off. They checked me and gave me medical attention for two weeks. They put me in a room by myself. The white, soft bed was the nicest one I had seen. I was shocked that this attention was all for me. I was exhausted – I truly needed that rest.

It was very quiet and peaceful there. The hospital room contained polished and very neat, old furniture. There was a picture on every wall. My window opened to the front of the building, and I could see everything in the camp from it, including the gate through which I had entered. I could also see Jean's building. I could watch his approach when he came to visit me to see how I was doing. Any time he came to see me, he never failed to say, "John, I am praying for you." All the nurses got to know him, so he could visit me any time he wanted. They knew he was a Christian, but I wasn't yet.

Jean told me that he had found a Romanian Baptist church and he was attending there. He described the members of the church and told me that they received him in love and with open arms. I knew this was bait to attract me to go with him, but I wasn't ready yet. Most of his visits were devoted to discussions about the Bible! I asked him if the women at the church were cute, but he didn't want to talk like that. Jean truly cared about me and I knew that. I never intended to offend him. He was so peaceful and spoke so calmly, especially now that he was out of Romania. His attitude had changed entirely, and he didn't talk about the past.

The people from Jean's church were mostly refugees. Their primary concern was to save enough money in Austria so they could send for their families. Many paid others to bring their wives and children out. After being in Austria for a few years, they were given asylum. They had the same rights as native Austrians. Jean's brothers and sisters from his church asked how he came to Austria, but he didn't have much to say; he just pointed to me. Then he explained my situation and what I had been through. They invited me to their church, but I still wasn't ready.

The rich food upset my stomach for the first few days. When I told the nurse about my stomach problems, she told the doctor. That afternoon, the doctor came to my room with the nurse and checked me again. He saw my big surgery scars. He was amazed. He asked me what had happened. I told him about my stress, my depression and my bleeding ulcer. After that, he took very good care of me. He gave me special medication that helped me to recover. I couldn't believe how much interest he showed in me. Ten days later, I was a new man. Every day the nurses brought me food to my room. They left the tray on a little cabinet. All I had to do was to get down, wash my face, sit on my bed, and eat. The only major problem was that I still couldn't understand them; I did not speak German, and none of them spoke Romanian.

One afternoon, one of the nurses came and brought me food and checked my papers. She informed me that I would be released in 4 more days. I was very happy to hear that news. I had been unable to talk to anyone, so I was anxious to go back to the camp to find other Romanians to talk to.

That same evening the nurse brought me a whole 6-pack of Coca-Cola cans. I had never had a soft drink before; I had never even heard of Coca-Cola. I knew about mineral water, lemonade, hot, sweet tea, coffee and hot chocolate, but not about Coke. I pulled one can out of the plastic collar and looked at the mysterious writing. I turned it around to examine the can, and then I realized I had to pull the metal tab to open it. When I opened the can, it popped and sprayed the bed and me. I knew I was in big trouble. I tried to wipe up the mess. When the nurse came and saw all the spots on my bed, she started laughing about it, and she could tell it was my first Coke, because I was wearing it. My first Coke, at age 30!

Before I left the hospital, the nurses brought me some clothes. I really needed clothes. I will never forget how well I was treated by the medical staff.

I moved back to the camp with Jean. I got to talk with lots of new Romanian people in the camp and share tales with them. My feet were well and my stomach was, too. I have had no more medical problems to this day.

The next day, we went back to the immigration office and I thanked the man in charge for everything he had done for us, and for his concern. Also, we told him we wanted asylum in Austria.

Though Jean and I were best friends, we did not have the same desires or dreams. We both wanted to leave, but for different countries. Jean was set on Canada, whilst I planned for Australia. Although we were free to travel, for the first days I stayed in camp. I had met other Romanian families. We talked endlessly about all the bad things the communist regime had done and the hard conditions there. For a while, I allowed myself to reflect on my past. All of us refugees had lots of harrowing stories, especially about the borders, the dangers and our journeys. They had been there too. All the Romanians were very friendly to Jean and me. They talked incessantly about their plans.

These new surroundings sent me into culture shock – new languages, new people, new cities and, of course, a new country. I had to learn German and the rules of their culture. I was like a new-born baby; I had to re-learn everything. I sure needed to, because my culture seemed backward compared with theirs.

Wandering the Streets of Vienna

WE WERE NOT RESTRICTED IN LEAVING the camp. Nobody said anything to us about it. On the first few trips I was asked for my identification because I was new in camp but, later on when the Austrian authorities knew me, I didn't have any problem. The authorities treated us very well. I knew my old life was behind me and I had to accept the changes day by day. I didn't know where to start. I was just getting over my paranoia when strangers looked at me. Slowly, I was adapting to Austria. I was learning what it was like to be normal.

This was about the middle of October 1988. I will never forget that October. While I had been in the infirmary, Jean had been spending every other day at his new church and had developed a strong relationship with the brothers and sisters. I was concerned about this. I began to leave the camp on short trips by myself, because Jean was gone most of the time. I explored the town of Transkirchen. I visited all the shops and little stores. I found a delightful cafe and started to hang out there.

The camp was about 5 minutes from the train station. The train station at Transkirchen was very small. A train left for Vienna every 40 minutes. Each train had 4 or 5 passenger cars. This time I got to ride inside. You couldn't miss the Vienna trains because they were red. Travel time from Transkirchen to Vienna was about 40 minutes. I got to see the local people up close, because the train stopped at lots of small towns. The passenger coaches were clean and comfortable. One passenger car was non-smoking. I hated that because I wanted to be with Jean, but he didn't smoke. I often rode the non-smoking car so we could carry on conversations. These red trains all terminated in Vienna, so all the passengers got off.

The Vienna train station was huge; I had never seen such a big train station; it had lots of tracks and terminals. The central terminal had two levels. We disembarked inside the second level. The big platform on the second level was covered in grey tiles. On the right was a waiting room, and offices were located on the left. The walls surrounding the waiting room were made of thick plate glass. The waiting room had benches around the walls and several round tables and chairs were at its centre. We normally walked downstairs to the lower level, where 10 cashiers sold tickets. Above the cashiers was a big, electronic train-scheduling board, with all the information about departures and arrivals. The board gave the time and number of each train and its terminal.

There were lots of people, lots of baggage, and lots of tourists. The train station was always filled with travellers. The lower level had a big restaurant and little speciality shops. Several of the doors were opened permanently at the entrance to the train station. There were also glass doors that opened automatically.

The flow of people was non-stop. There was a bus station integrated into the train station. The buses fed into a big, bustling boulevard. The pavements were asphalt, but the city streets were mostly cobblestone. The roads were old, but then the city was old, too. The traffic on major roads parted like the sea around the red trams that served downtown. Vienna had an oval belt of wide boulevards called the Ringstrasse. I called it the Ring, because most of the Viennese people called it that. There were lots of modern apartments, where the majority of the Viennese lived. Most of the buildings in central Vienna were antique, some hundreds of years old, and full of art. We discovered the Kartplatz, which was the heart of all subways. That was the terminus where all the subways crossed. Everything was underground, including many little shops with fast food, newspapers, telephone booths, book stores, jewellery, tobacco, and much, much more!

My favourite subway trip was to the Schönbrunn Palace. This palace had the biggest park in Vienna. It was four subway stops from the Kartplatz. Some outlying subway stations were level with the ground and some were subterranean. The entire system was electric, and incredibly fast. People sat around the sides of the subway cars. In the middle stood the "strap-hangers", people holding on to the straps suspended from the ceilings. The subway cars had windows, but the lights were always turned on.

When we got off the subway at Schönbrunn Palace, we walked about 300 metres to get to the park gate. The park was fenced. Inside, about 100 metres from the gate, was the palace itself, built for the Empress Maria Theresa. It was simply huge, like Versailles. A portion of the palace was a museum. The palace had 1400 rooms, but most of it was closed to the public. It was 3 storeys high, and yellow, covered with terra cotta tiles. On either side of the main entrance were 25 statues of the Hapsburg ruling families. The place was full of antiques and art. We had never seen such an ornate building. But I was more interested in the gardens than the palace. I walked many times through the park in front of the building. It was a huge park, full of all kinds of different flowers, of every colour and shade. There were gorgeous topiary gardens as well. The turf was very green, and faultlessly cut. There were benches and paths and statues everywhere.

If I walked on the left side of the Schönbrunn Palace I would see the beautiful high trees and, between them, small bushes trimmed neatly. About 300 metres from the Palace was a beautiful artesian fountain. It was wide, and about 70 centimetres deep. In its centre was a beautiful statue. Around the fountain was a very wide promenade. The fountain was made of red marble and brown tile. Around it were benches, where I routinely camped. The sound of the water was always relaxing and charming. The fountain area was elevated and, from there, I could see parts of Vienna in the distance. It was a very beautiful area, and I will never forget it. The park was always busy with tourists, especially children. I remember so many, many times I walked in this park. It was a place that gave me peace. Most of the time I walked alone. I did not talk with anybody when I was there. I kept to myself and admired the beauty of that place. My mind rested, especially from the things of the past. Jean knew it was my favourite place, but I never actually explained to him what it meant to me. I felt as free as a bird when I walked slowly around it.

Another beautiful place, also one of my favourites, was the River Danube. I had a special, private place on its bank where I went to sit for long hours, just watching the water flow. I didn't swim, because the water was turbid. I just walked on the shore barefoot, wading in the shoreline puddles. I could hear and see lots of different birds there. The Danube was about 600 metres wide and very deep. It was also very busy – large commercial ships and barges travelled it constantly, besides lots of small, private boats. There were many riverbank parks. Some were secluded, but most of them were full of people on blankets. Lots of families cooked and played together in the parks.

Another favourite place was at Kartnerstrasse, which was between the Opera House and St Stephen's Cathedral. It is the geographical centre of Vienna, as well as its the banking and commercial centre. I walked up and down that street many times. That was where the rich patricians walked. On Kartnerstrasse there were also concert halls, art galleries, museums and theatres.

The most elegant shops, with high-fashion clothing, were located on Kartnerstrasse. Most Austrians wore clothing much like that worn in the USA, but the Viennese are different; they are very elegant and sophisticated. In front of the Opera House, men appear in white tie and tails, women in long gowns. On special holidays, they wear their traditional costumes. Men may wear a green-trimmed, grey wool suit consisting of a coat and knickerbockers. Women may wear a peasant costume called a dirndl. It consists of a blouse, a white corset worn over the blouse and laced up the front like a bustier, and a full, brightly-coloured skirt and apron. When I first saw them wearing those kinds of clothing, I thought they were tourists from another country, but then I realized they were just their traditional folk costumes.

Everything was very expensive there. However, the real attractions for me were the many German restaurants with the very best German food. Oh, those bakery smells... and I can't forget the coffee-houses and cafés! Black coffee is a tradition in Vienna, as is a sweet chocolate cake named "Sachertorte". Viennese traditionally serve these together. They love good food. Most of the meats I ate there were beef, chicken, pork and seafood. I got addicted to potatoes, noodles and German dumplings. Oh, that sweet smell of potatoes mixed with Viennese cheese and butter; I'd never had such food! It was all new to me, but they were good and very tasty. Austrian food was a mixture of German and Hungarian cooking. The Viennese (and I) love to drink beer or wine with a meal. Excellent red or white wine was imported from Italy.

I always stopped at every bakery. It was the cheapest entertainment I knew. I got to see all kinds of colourful breads. The designs were fantastic – the bakers must have been artists as well. The delicious cake and pastries made by Austrian bakers are very famous. In each bakery I visited, I offered my services to make sure nothing got stale. My favourite bread was German rye. I ate it constantly, as sandwiches or for breakfast with salamis and cheese. There were lots of places I enjoyed, but my greatest attraction was to the restaurants and good food, especially Viennese ice cream, in all kinds of flavours, covered with melted chocolate. And that baked chicken with a strong garlic aroma! That was one of my favourites. I had never had a whole chicken roasted, but I did in Vienna. Also, the Viennese garden salad; oh, I still can see the big platters with cheese dressing. All these things were new to me. I never knew such things existed. I soon felt like I belonged in Austria. The Austrians were really happy and friendly. You could read it in their faces.

Another attractive place where I spent many hours was St Stephen's Cathedral. It is huge, very beautiful and very tall. The Cathedral is one of Vienna's most important buildings, and can be seen from afar. It was built in about 1400, but actually took several hundred years to complete. It is full of paintings and statuary. It has a huge iron-and-hardwood door at the entrance. The beautiful, shiny benches were made from hardwood, with leather seats and with kneelers. There were many large, iron chandeliers on chains hanging from the ceiling. The transept was very high, the walls were frescoed, and the windows were beautiful stained glass. Statues were everywhere. On the altar were small crosses. The altar was for communion and mass. It was covered with white linen embroidered with a big cross. To the rear of the altar was a big, iron cross with Jesus Christ. Hundreds of lights reflected from it. To the side of the cross were a statue of the Virgin Mary and a statue of St Joseph. Huge columns lined the transept and nave. Votive candles burned constantly. On the top of the Cathedral were 3 huge, brass bells.

Ninety percent of Austrians are Roman Catholic, but they were quite tolerant of other religions. There were no restraints on visiting St Stephen's, and it was perpetually packed with tourists. Lots of pictures were taken inside and outside the Cathedral. Many languages could be heard at a single sitting in any café in town. Many foreign tour groups walked together to talk and sightsee. Vienna is the most beautiful city I have ever seen, and it was my favourite city while I was at Transkirchen;

at least, until I left the camp to go to Hohe-Wand. I spent a lot of time in Vienna and often travelled on the trains and subways.

I had no problems in the camp with the Austrian authorities. If I asked a question of someone, I got answered in a proper manner and with polite respect. The camp was one big family, especially for the Romanians. We hung around each other most of the time. We also helped each other with many kinds of needs. In a short time, I had lots of friends in Austria. We all had different dreams, but really wanted the same thing: friendship. It was wonderful to be with the people in that camp. Nobody argued or fought. We drank, but we were happy drunks. Most of the time, I left for Vienna in the morning and stayed there most of the day. I was back at the camp by 7 p.m. each night. I ate supper and took a shower and, after that, I lay down on my bed to rest. I saw new places – streets, markets, small shops, and much more each day. Romania slowly receded from my daily consciousness; I quit reliving my escape. I slowly shifted my focus to the future and enjoying the present. Standing in that Austrian refugee camp, I had more things and more hope and better prospects for the future than I had ever had in Romania. I had no worries. The camp fed me excellently 3 times a day and, if I was hungry between meals, all I had to do was ask the personnel.

My primary tasks were to become accustomed to the people around me and to learn German. German came along very slowly for me. I had no daily responsibilities. It was time I needed to get comfortable with the freedom. Time went quickly. The longer I stayed at the camp, the more I learned new things. It was a challenge for me, especially confronting so many unexpected things.

I slowed my travelling because of the cold weather of October. Winter changed everything. The place wasn't that busy any more, and the parks changed as well. The leaves, grass and flowers slowly disappeared. I still remember the people around our camp who brought us more clothes. Never in Romania had I been so well-clothed. So many trousers, shoes and jackets! I couldn't believe it. I cried. I knew even better was to come. I still continued going to Kartnerstrass, no matter how the weather was, because of my favourite bread.

Christmas and New Year at the camp were special. I had a new family. I still remember that time very well. I had no money or other possessions, but I was free and well-fed. That counted more than anything else did in this world. We were all waiting to be transferred to other places. Most of the immigrants were eventually transferred from the camp. Everyone was awaiting asylum in another country.

I started to reflect more on learning German. The language wasn't hard but, because of my pronunciation, I was reticent to speak. I had plenty of time to study the language, and I knew I had to learn, because I could not communicate otherwise. Early on I was really at a disadvantage, because I could not understand the news, or other radio or TV programmes. When I went into the stores, the employees wanted to talk with me and be friendly but, when they saw I didn't speak German, they walked away and watched every move I made. I wanted, and needed, to find a job – anything to make my own money so that I could help myself and others in need.

Searching for Work

One of the reasons I wanted to start work while I was in Austria and still in the process of learning a new language, was that I was worried about my "second family", the Constantinescus, who were back in Romania and existing in poverty. I was especially worried about my friend, Magdalena, who had brought me the Bible. I knew she had many needs, especially at her age. She was anxious about lots of things just like I was, and I wanted to show love and care for her through my actions, not just in words. But it wasn't just her. The Constantinescu family consisted of both parents and 9 little children. They all lived in one small apartment – all of them. I really don't know how they managed, but that was reality.

I wanted to do something to help them. That was why finding a job was such an urgent matter. I knew the other little children needed clothes and some extra food on their table. I promised to every little one that I would not forget them when I got to Austria – I had to keep my promise. They stood beside me in Romania when I got out of the hospital. When I got out of the hospital I stayed at Magdalena's father's farm, where he raised pigs. Most of the time I was there, watching and working. It was good for me to stay there, rather than be out on the streets. I had been happy for that. Magdalena's father had worked for many, many years as a coal-miner, but now he was in retirement. It had been hard for me to accept that kind of privation then, but there was no other choice.

The family had lived in the apartment, while Constantinescu and I had lived at the farm. It was convenient for me, because the police didn't know where we were. I told the Constantinescu family not to tell anybody, not even to mention my name! Chris,

my partner on my first escape attempt to the border, was part of the family and the authorities wanted to separate us. Magdalena brought us food to the farm, so I did not move around too much, especially because of my healing surgery scars. The farm barrack was on a hill from which I could survey most of the town. I could sit on its roof and watch the town, roads and surrounding mountains. It was a beautiful view and it made me feel secure, but I dwelled on the city view to make sure no police were on the road and coming my way. The hills there were covered with forests, as were the mountains, apart from their bald tops. I could see the River Jiul flowing slowly down in quietness. There wasn't much noise from the city, because there wasn't much traffic. I just sat in the sun and really enjoyed the view of the mountains.

The Constantinescu family were supported by their Pentecostal Church. There were many church members who came to visit with Constantinescu at the farm barrack. Of course, having such visitors led me to talk more than I should. They were good people and were genuinely concerned about me, but I was proud and didn't want, or need, their attention. I was focused on secrecy and escape. I did not want to talk about God and Jesus either, especially to them at that time. They tried to comfort me, but the only consolation I wanted was freedom. I didn't have anything against them, but I wasn't ready for their teaching and help. I was relying on myself and I did not accept them.

Anyway, some of the church members came every single day to Constantinescu's farm and tried to include me in their religious discussions. One day, I told Constantinescu that I had to move on, because the "holy rollers" kept trying to hammer on my head again! Sure enough, he understood. The next time they came, he quickly told them that I was deeply disturbed and needed peace and quiet. I remembered all of these things as I reflected on the Constantinescus as my second family. I truly did not understand all of their kindness towards me. I remember that he kept saying, "John, one day you'll understand, when the Lord visits you!" I didn't understand what he was trying to tell me, but I didn't ask him what it meant. I pretended that I understood and I was in agreement with him. I kept asking myself what it meant for the Lord to visit me. But I moved on with other things of more immediate importance to me. This family was special to me. I love them all. I will never forget all the good things they did for me.

Christmas and New Year passed in no time at Transkirchen. It was a cold and windy January. The roads were covered with ice and a white mantle of snow and ice covered everything. The trees had new forms, especially without their leaves. I was clothed and shod pretty well and was able to face the white winter and even enjoy it. As I later sat in my Austrian refugee camp, I realized that no one should ever be in need of warm clothes. Very different from Romania! Most of the time at the camp, I sat in my dorm with my new friends or lay in bed, resting. I eventually recuperated from my surgery and escape, but I still had to work on my sour attitude. I still found it difficult to trust people – it didn't matter how nice they were towards me.

Hohe Wand – High Wall

THE LORD GOD WAS WITH US. After we had been at the Transkirchen refugee camp almost 5 months, we were again summoned to the Austrian immigration authorities. It was a welcome relief, better than sitting around licking my psychological wounds and my surgery scars. I was ready for change. Jean became frightened because he thought they might transfer us far away from Vienna. Then he would have no more access to his new playground. I told him that he should pray about it, because that was how he would respond to me when I was making some decision; a little Christian sarcasm.

We were summoned to the immigration office. The place was packed with lots of people who were there for the same reason. The immigration interviewer already knew who I was. He had also checked on Jean. He told us we would be transferred from Transkirchen – the main camp – to a smaller camp near Graz. I was thrilled to hear that. As long as it wasn't back to Romania, I was happy. He asked us if we accepted this and, of course, we did, without question. We were not worried any more. I knew things were only improving.

They transferred us after lunch. At one p.m. a man called our names. He was a tall Austrian, with our papers in his hand. He asked if we had baggage. I nodded and showed him two small, plastic trash-bags with our clothes in. That was more than enough to carry all of my possessions.

Our driver motioned for us and some others to follow him, and we walked out to the parking lot. We stopped at a large van, which he opened for us. There were many immigrants leaving the camp with us – 5 Romanians and a Polish couple. Before I realized it, we were flying down the autobahn going south to Graz. Everything was moving very fast. The autobahn had no speed limit. There were 5 lanes each way.

Traffic was heavy as we left Transkirchen. I got quiet and just enjoyed the spectacle of autobahn travel. The autobahn didn't go through the cities or towns, only between them. We zipped past private houses, forests and open fields. A 20-cm blanket of white snow covered everything around, but the autobahn was dry. I was amazed to see the sculpted earthworks at the exits. You could exit going 60 km/h on a curved and banked ramp, and you didn't even have to slow down. The exits were very wide and in good repair. The roadway was perfectly smooth. My head bobbed from left to right to see everything.

After 3 hours we arrived in Graz, a very big city. I saw lots of tall buildings and apartment blocks. The streets were old, as were most of the buildings around us. We didn't go through the city centre, because of heavy traffic. We circled on a perimeter highway. After 30 minutes, the van pulled into a motel. I thought that maybe the driver had stopped for a rest break, but then I saw the Polish couple get out of the van. I was surprised. I asked myself if they were to stay in the motel. I had previously heard people talking about how the Austrian authorities might locate refugees in different hotels, motels and houses. This would have been a luxury for us, being just poor immigrants. I thought it must cost lots of money. The motel was a huge building. It was 10 floors high and blue. It had a big parking lot all around it. In front were two big glass doors. Some of our crew got out of the van and said their good-byes and hugged. I didn't understand what was happening, but then I was just along for the ride.

Shortly, we were back on the autobahn and speeding away from Graz. After a while, one of the remaining passengers began talking with the driver. He was a very friendly man, who laughed most of the time. One of the passengers asked him about the job prospects in Austria. The driver told us that there was plenty of work; Austrians were too spoiled to do menial jobs. When I heard that, I was thrilled and encouraged. I was ready for a job. I was already making plans. The rest of the conversations didn't interest me. I knew I would be able to work. Although I understood much of what our driver said, I could not yet respond in German.

Our Alpine Resettlement Camp

WE TRAVELLED FOR ANOTHER TWO HOURS and then once again left the autobahn. I saw the big sign as we exited. The city was called Viener Neustadt. When we got to the main street, we again turned and drove out of the town towards the mountain. We passed many commercial businesses and motels. We passed another small town without stopping. Then we arrived at the tiny town of Stollhof. I saw a couple of grocery stores, a bar, post office and other little small businesses on the main road. After passing through Sotho, we turned right off the main road.

Then I saw the sign bearing the name of our destination: Hohe Wand, meaning "high wall". It was on the top of a mountain. The road curved higher and higher, and went through a big pine forest. I had seen the mountain from the autobahn, but I didn't know it was our destination. The altitude of the mountain was about 3000 metres (almost 10000 feet). As we passed through the forest heading up the mountain, all we saw were dense pine and hardwood forests. It was a very dangerous drive, inclined at 40 degrees. There was no traffic. On the right side, at the edge, was a very strong barrier of steel bands to protect cars from driving over the side.

After 20 minutes, we arrived at the top on a flat field. I saw a huge house, and then I saw a second house, bigger than any of the other houses. It was under construction. The van kept going and ascended to yet another plateau on the big mountain. It was 7 o'clock in the evening and it was already dark. I knew we were close to the house where we would be staying, and that our trip was over. The van pulled up to a huge house – the new home for us 5 Romanians. The house was 3 storeys tall. The second storey had a balcony all around the outside of the house. It was tan brick and surrounded with big pine trees. I couldn't see more, because we walked inside. A tall Austrian man stood at the door and shook our hands as we entered. Then a blonde woman greeted us with a warm smile and open arms. She was inside the room with another older couple and two little girls. They were like one big family. We all tried to talk with each other, and make introductions.

The owner was Rodney, the blonde woman was his wife, and the little girls were their children. Rodney was about 32 years old, his wife about 5 years younger. They were Austrian. His wife was originally from Poland. The older couple was Herr Huver and his wife. They were Rodney's parents. They were a very happy family. Herr Huver and his wife hugged me and showed lots of interest in me. They listened to everything I said when I tried to speak to them. They wanted to make sure they understood what I was asking for. Many times, I wondered how someone could love me as they did. I didn't understand, because I still thought of myself as the problem. My mentality was still Romanian.

I became special to Herr Huver and his wife. I did not know why, but they treated me much better than the others – they treated me as if I belonged to them. We were all treated well and with respect. There was nothing in this world I would do to offend them. I saw them as my father and mother, which is how much I cared for them. I had so much sympathy for them, especially because they were older people. The Romanian couple spoke very little German and I spoke none, so I felt bad because I wanted to thank them and I couldn't.

We sat for about 30 minutes in that big room where we had made our introductions. They called it their "restaurant". The room was full of tables and chairs and also there were benches round the walls. The tables were covered with beautiful floral cloths. On the top of each table was a big piece of plastic for protection. Along the front wall was a bar, where they served beer, cigarettes and snacks. The floors were brown ceramic tile. It was neat and everything was in place. The bar had a Coca Cola machine. They served soft drinks, too. The walls were papered with beautiful patterns. The ceiling was beamed and the plaster between was painted. Three chandeliers hung from the ceiling. From the dining room, we walked down a short hall, where we saw another community room and the kitchen. Next to that was Rodney's apartment, where he stayed with his family. On the left inside were two separate bathrooms. The hall and the stairs were carpeted in red. Everything was very neat and in its place.

I talked with the other Romanians and came to know them better. We talked for another 30 minutes at the table, and everyone told their personal stories.

Rodney knew we were coming and would be hungry; he was expecting us, because the immigration authority had called him. They brought a big basket with sliced German rye bread. There was one big pot, with vegetable soup with pork. It was red and it smelled very good. Another pot contained boiled potatoes, with seasoning and parsley on top. Two small pots contained more vegetables. One had green beans and the other had mushrooms. There was a platter with meatballs. There were more immigrants in the house, who ate with us. They came for supper and we met them all. There were 3 other couples and 4 single, young men. All of them were Hungarian. Rodney and his wife served us all. Jean gave thanks to God for the food, which was perfectly spiced and seasoned. I ate the first bowl in no time. Immediately, Rodney asked if I would like some more, and I accepted. After I had eaten the soup, they handed me another plate with green beans, whole potatoes, mushrooms and 3 meatballs. It was like a restaurant. After that, I felt like a new man. It was like a celebration. I was in another world. I had no words to thank them for opening their beautiful home up to us.

After supper, we talked with Rodney and asked him all kinds of questions. My first question was about jobs. Rodney assured me that I would be able to find one in no time. That encouraged me.

Finally, Rodney showed us our rooms. We walked out of our "little restaurant" and went upstairs. The steps were metal and wood. The room was spacious. There were 3 full-size beds, little cabinets, a table and two chairs. On the right-hand side was another door to our own shower and toilet. The floor was covered with thick, grey carpet and the shower had light-brown tiles. When I sat down on one of the beds, I felt the softness of the mattress. That was the best mattress I ever had. It felt like the mattress from the medical infirmary at Transkirchen, where I had stayed for two weeks. I'd been sleeping on cots for so long that I had forgotten what real mattresses felt like. There were pictures on the walls, too. A big green curtain that ran floor-to-ceiling covered the window. It had a balcony, which we could access from a side door.

Our room had an electric heater. I chose the bed closest to the window, because I smoked. Jean and another Romanian, named Tony, didn't. I had to respect them. I showered quickly after dinner and went to bed. I was very tired after so many hours of travel. It was quiet in our room. Morpheus carried me away quietly.

I awoke the next day at about 7 a.m. I changed clothes and walked downstairs to get something to eat. I said, "Guten morgen," – I was learning – one of the few German phrases I knew, and they served me breakfast. I got a big cup of coffee. On the table was a little glass jar with a lid on top – it was the sugar. Also, in another little cup, was milk. I ate fried eggs, German bread with butter and two slices of salami with cheese. Then, after 3 sandwiches and coffee, I was full. Of course, my favourite part of breakfast was my fried eggs. Frau Huver fried me 4 eggs. I explained to her as best I could how I'd like them. This breakfast was a pure luxury. We hadn't had many eggs in Romania. The chickens were very skinny, so they ran very fast. We never had eggs by themselves in Romania. Most eggs were used in cooking breads, cakes and sauces.

I didn't see much scenery outside because a thick fog had rolled up the valley, so I went back to my room and napped until the weather broke and we could see clearly outside. When it did, it was about one p.m. and I saw a very beautiful, sunny day from the big balcony window. My first clear, unobstructed view of the surrounding area was a startling panorama. I walked out onto the balcony, and I could see for ever. The house was perched on the edge of a cliff near the top of the mountain, so it gave us a sense of isolation, seclusion and peace. Below I saw many little towns, as well as Viener Neustadt. It was a beautiful scene. I could trace out in my mind all the little roads and switchbacks we had taken the day before. I sat there on the balcony for many hours. The beauty of the place was exhilarating. I couldn't name all the towns at first, but I learned them in no time. I knew I had to go and search for a job.

Another beautiful view was the big autobahn from Vienna to Graz. There was a continuous line of ants on both sides of the autobahn: Mercedes ants, Volkswagen ants, Audi ants, and many more. Night-time was even more beautiful, because the ants on the autobahn lit up and became white and red fireflies. Between 9 and 11 p.m. was the best time to watch the heavy traffic. After 12 o'clock, it slowed down and then the mountainside houses and resorts lit up.

The distance between houses was about 400 metres. The style of the houses varied from region to region. Valley houses are usually farmhouses with attached or included barns. Many farmers and village families live in these large, family homes. The majority of farmers raise their own pigs, chickens, horses and cows. But the mountain houses were different – made of stone, with steep roofs. They were built almost like castles in order to withstand the harsh weather. Everyone, whether they lived in the valley or the mountains, has a shiny, well-tended car. Austrians are nothing if not meticulous.

I never saw such unpredictable and changeable weather as in Hohe Wand. The nights were very cold. The icy roads were very dangerous, but I stayed inside until it warmed up a little bit. The mountains were always snow-capped. Mornings were very foggy. The sun never shone until at least 10 a.m. Sometimes it would rain for several weeks on end. Most of the time it was cold. Summertime was short, but with beautiful weather. The humidity was always high and the vegetation was always lush, with a lot of mushrooms. I never saw such high grass or tall gardens. The rock formations were clean because of the rain.

Jean and I sat around and about a month passed. We strove to learn German so we would be able to talk with our neighbours. I started to read my Bible, because I saw Jean reading his. I felt ashamed – I didn't want him to think I was ignoring his good example. In all this time, Frau Huver offered to help us with the language. I started to trust her, and the rest of the camp. It took me a long time to smile, especially at strangers. I didn't know you were supposed to smile at strangers, because in my country that overture was dangerous. I had been conditioned by years of fear, repression and rejection in Romania. Openness wasn't easy to accept. Psychologically, I took a long time to heal and, besides that, I still didn't really understand that I was free. But Frau Huver understood me. I still had to work on myself, my sour attitude, and especially on my short temper. She was like a mother to me. I told her as best I could that I had a mother who never told me she loved me, and she died a few years ago...I remember that, during that time, there were lots of long German words that I could not understand. I would go to the kitchen to her and point to the word in my dictionary. She would stop and give me her full attention and lots of good explanations. She took time with me and had lots of patience. I still remember the day when she asked me if I went to church. When I heard that, I could not answer. I said, "I read the Bible," but she was not satisfied with that answer. After that, I started to pray with Jean. I let him pray because I didn't know what to say. He read the Bible and I listened. Sometimes he asked me if I understood. Immediately, I answered that I did, but I really didn't understand many of the things from the Bible.

Working in Hohe Wand

THE TIME WAS GOING BY FAST, but Jean and I spent it learning the most important German words first: food, work, bathroom, and so on. Learning German was our biggest task. We started walking around in our neighbourhood to see the place and where we could find work and make some money. When someone from our neighbourhood talked to us we shook our heads, pretending to understand, but we didn't. Then Jean and I repeated between ourselves everything that had been said, as we attempted to comprehend. The people around us showed so much kindness and respect, they treated us like family. We nodded and greeted everyone we met, even strangers. Walking around constantly, people got to know us and we fitted into the neighbourhood in no time. We found occasional small jobs and we were happy making a little money. The basic unit of currency was the schilling, which is smaller than the US dollar.

We never walked too far, because we didn't want to get lost. There were lots of forests there and the roads all looked alike. Anyway, I soon adapted. I began accepting the changes inside of me as well.

Within two months, I had picked up a basic vocabulary. I began to speak German. I could understand most conversation, but my problem was that I couldn't speak it well yet. By concentrating on learning German, worry and depression left me. I began to actually feel the ordeal was over. I was preparing to start a new life.

I kept returning to the second house we had seen the day we first arrived. I knew the owner must need help, because the house was obviously unfinished. I thought that, if I didn't understand what the owner said, Jean would. So that way, the owner could see that we had made some improvement by speaking his language. The house was about 3 kilometres away from where we lived, and it was plain that the house was incomplete. We kept going there looking for work. We knew that "first come, first served" was how it worked. We walked day after day and we looked around the house, but nobody showed up. Each time we stayed for an hour. The house was a massive alpine lodge. It was 3 storeys tall and had a 4-car garage.

At the beginning of March, we took another walk that way, not even thinking someone might be there. We walked through our neighbourhood and found ourselves before the unfinished hulk. When we drew near the house, we saw something suspicious.

A red car was parked at the side of the house, in front of the garage. When I saw it, my legs went weak. I knew I had to practise what German I had learned; I was insecure, but I had to try. Anyhow, we stopped beside the red car. The owner was a heavy-set man about 6 feet tall and in his 60s. As we approached, we greeted him. He greeted us back. He stared at us and let us speak first. I read on his face compassion and kindness toward us. I spoke very slowly and, sure enough, he understood that we were looking for work. He asked if we knew construction work. We replied, "No," but we promised that we would learn from him. He was pleased with our answer and hired us on the spot for a short task. Immediately, we accepted. I couldn't believe it. My mind started to fly in so many different directions. Jean told me that his prayers had been answered, and I told him not to stop praying (I was joking with him). I was thrilled, because I would be able to help the Constantinescu family and, of course, Magdalena. I knew they needed my help desperately and I had to keep my promise to them.

Our new boss didn't talk much, but Jean and I worked hard to be accepted. We told him we were Romanian, and I told him where we now lived. He knew Rodney, so he trusted us more. We worked 4 hours that day. He received two or three dump trucks of topsoil and we had to smooth it out around the house. We also removed the big rocks, because he planned to put sod in the yard. Of course, he paid us on the spot, and he said that he could come and pick us up in the morning, but I only understood the part about "in the morning." The part about being picked up I had misunderstood. We decided to tell nobody about our good fortune.

The next day, we awoke at 6 a.m. and walked to the construction site. We arrived at 7 a.m., but nobody was there. We decided to wait for the owner. We sat around for another two hours. We were not hungry, because Frau Huver had cooked us breakfast, early. We had told her that we wanted to leave early in the morning, so she made us a big breakfast.

Finally, we saw a taxi pull in towards the garages. We ran and welcomed our boss with a smile. Immediately, we took some paper bags from the car and took them inside the house. He had construction materials, and another two bags with drinks and food.

He smiled back at us and tried to ask us when we had arrived. We told him at 7 a.m. Then he knew that we had not understood what he had said the day before. The problem was that he spoke a different dialect, not Viennese. Jean and I had big problems understanding this dialect. After he had repeated himself many times, I understood exactly what he had meant. This time, I realized that he had told us that he would pick us up at 9 a.m. From that day on, he always repeated himself until we understood exactly what he was saying. As a matter of fact, he told us that he wanted to make sure we understood him from now on.

I started to call him "boss". I read his face and he was pleased. Jean and I worked about 5 hours. After that he said he had to go to work himself. There was lots of work to do there, but he didn't leave us there because, very understandably, he didn't trust us yet . Also, we didn't realize that he owned the taxi company – we thought the taxi he had arrived in belonged to someone else. He gave me 150 schillings and then took us back to our home. We were amazed at his generosity and kindness towards us. We thanked him. Before he left, he told us, for the second time, to be ready for tomorrow morning. He was coming at 9 a.m.

We were thankful for the work and the money, but we had a double language problem with our new "boss". We didn't speak German very well and, on top of that, he spoke a new, unfamiliar dialect. Jean and I had learned German around Vienna. Here, in Hohe Wand, it was a much different dialect, with many different pronunciations. But, this time, we both understood what he said. So, "boss" got in his Volvo 740 taxi, turned around and disappeared. After that, we walked into the house and Rodney told us that the man who had just left us was a millionaire. We weren't concerned with that. We were just happy for the jobs. Over lunch, I told Rodney and his wife of our good fortune. Immediately, Rodney offered to go to the grocery store to buy food to send back to the Contstantinescu family, in Romania. We continued our work with our boss and, a week later, I sent the Constantinescu family (in Magdalena's name) a 15-kg package. It contained coffee, blue jeans, sweets for the little ones, and other beautiful clothes for Magdalena. Coffee was scarce and expensive in Romania. It was fast money; it could be sold to help the whole family. Magdalena had been writing to me, so Jean and I were up on the family gossip and we also knew what they needed.

Jean and I grew as close as brothers. We prayed and talked about the Lord Jesus Christ together. We were happy. We worked hard for our taxi company owner, sometimes 5 days a week or, sometimes, only two days, depending on how busy our boss was. That first evening, when we went to supper, the Hungarian couple asked if we had found jobs. I told them that we had. Then I described the magnificent house under construction and its owner, my new boss. It turned out that they had been there and also asked for work but my boss refused them. I like to think that God just wanted Jean and me to work there, that it was his plan all along. I am convinced that slowly, our prayers were being heard and answered. But, unfortunately, the Hungarians became jealous of us and they stopped speaking with us for a while. We prayed for them – as Jean instructed me – and things got better. They became our friends again. I started to believe and trust in Jean to help me with the Bible. He did his utmost to help me understand the word of God. He also helped me to relax and trust God.

> "Trust in the Lord with all thine heart;
> and lean not unto thine own understanding.
> In all thy ways acknowledge him, and he
> shall direct thy paths."   (Proverbs 3:5, 6)

At that moment, I still had problems understanding my Bible, especially Proverbs. It seemed like another language to me, but my friend, Jean, assured me by repetition until I got some kind of glimmer.

My thinking began to change. I released the anger and bad attitude I previously had toward others. I was reading the Bible daily with Jean. He showed me lots of kindness, and took the time to answer all of my questions about the Bible and a Christian life. He was very patient with me, because he considered me his "big brother." He was concerned about me. During that time, I stopped many of my bad habits. I was determined to learn to live a Christian life. The more I read, the more I understood my old mistakes – lying, cheating, stealing, fighting, and a lack of trust in men. I hoped that I had put these things behind me.

Our boss was wonderful, but I still didn't know his name. He never said his name so that either of us could actually understand it. And, since he paid us in cash, we never had any written record of who was our benefactor, or friend.

Two weeks later, my friend, Jean, got a telephone call from Vienna. The church where he was a member asked him if he wanted to come and stay in Vienna. Of course, he accepted. When he came back to our room, I saw a brightly smiling, shining face upon him and he was giving thanks to God. I asked him, "What is it?" He told me that the brothers from the Baptist Romanian Church wanted him there. When I heard that, I couldn't speak for a moment. After that shock, I said, "Go for it."

The next day, about 8 o'clock in the morning, two members of the church came to pick him up. I got to meet them. One was Peter and the other was George. Both of them lived in Vienna. They gave me a warm invitation to their church, and I said I would come one day. The next time my boss came to get us for work, I walked by myself to his car. He asked about Jean. I explained that Jean's church members had asked him to move to Vienna to be closer to the congregation. I said that the church would provide for him. Now it was just me; I was alone.

After Jean moved to Vienna, my boss began to trust me with more responsibility. He gave me a set of keys. I did whatever he said, cleaning or construction. In a very short time, I learned a lot about construction from him. I did the work as he wanted, and he was very pleased with my careful work. When he didn't have time to come, he called me and told me what he wanted me to do. When the job was done, I called and told him how the work had gone, and then I went back home. He was very satisfied.

I was quickly becoming fluent in German. I didn't have much problem understanding, but it still took me time to translate from German to Romanian and then back to German again. I could almost carry on a regular conversation with my boss. I learned his dialect, and it was easy for me. My boss asked me a lot of questions about my country and, of course, I was glad to tell him what was going on there. He couldn't believe the worst of it, but he accepted what I told him. He made provision for me to have food and soft drinks at work. And, when he came, he always brought my favourite sandwiches and my favourite drinks. My boss didn't like to see me smoking, especially knowing that I had had surgery on my stomach. He was concerned about me and tried his best to help me stop. I never understood his exceptional kindness and compassion towards me. I never knew, in my country, a man as devoted as he was.

Two weeks after Jean left, our other roommate, Tom, went to another city because he didn't like the mountains. Now I was by myself in one big room; I felt very lonely. Jean was gone and nobody was around for me to talk to. My boss initially worried about Jean, but then he relaxed because he knew the church was supporting Jean's needs. We kept up our friendship by calling each other. Gradually, I got used to staying by myself.

Searching for an Austrian Church Home

IT WAS ALMOST THE END of March 1989 when some of my Romanian friends, Nicu and his wife, Ella, stopped me and asked if I wanted to go to church. I felt that God was calling me to His house. Actually, I was looking for a local Romanian church, but I could not refuse Nicu and Ella, because they had seen Jean and me together and they knew Jean loved the Lord. Also, Jean talked with them a few times and felt they knew the Lord, too. I asked them if they knew a Romanian church around. They said, "We know a very good American church." They wanted to take me to an American Protestant church in Vienna. I wondered how in the world I would understand English, when I didn't know German very well yet. Then, they tried to explain to me that there was a man who spoke many languages, including Romanian. I had no answer to that, so I said, "Well, let me think about it."

I went back to my room and lay down to rest and get ready for the next day. As I lay in bed, I conjured up visions of all kinds of churches, but I did not know what it meant. The next evening, I called Jean and told him about it. We didn't know what my dreams had meant, but he said that I needed to find a church: "Choose a church you like and stay there." He didn't insist that I come to his church. My choice was harder than it first appeared; I had no experience with churches and I didn't know the Bible well. The church invitation of my friend, Nicu, remained with me. I was praying about it even as I continued my routines.

At the end of March, I came home from work one day to eat and rest for a while. As I lay in bed, I heard a knock at my door. It was Nicu, to invite me to his room. I was suspicious, but then he explained that some of his church friends were coming, and they wanted me to meet them. I accepted.

169

When I walked in, I met a man about my size who had a trimmed beard. Ella, Nicu's wife, was talking with a woman. She was obviously oriental (Chinese, I think). The two strangers sat on Nicu and Ella's bed – there wasn't a lot of furniture. When they saw me, they both smiled. They were introduced as Pastor Rob and his wife, Mary. We all shook hands, then we sat and chatted for a while. I learned Rob's full name was Robert Prokob. He asked me if I knew the Lord. I said, "Yes," but I didn't. I was reading and praying, but I never called on Jesus Christ to be my Lord and Saviour.

> "That if thou shalt confess with thy mouth
> the Lord Jesus, and shalt believe in thine
> heart that God hath raised him from the
> dead, thou shalt be SAVED.
> For with the heart man believeth unto
> righteousness: and with the mouth confession is
> made unto salvation." (Romans 10:9-10)

Later on, I found out these things at Rob's church. When he invited me to his church, I explained that I had no car and no transportation. Up in the mountains, everyone had a car but me. I told him that I would try to come. After they left, I went back to my room and thought about it. I went downstairs and called Jean, and I told him what had happened. Immediately, he said, "Why don't you try?"

The next Sunday, Nicu, his wife and I decided to go to Rob's church. The church service started at 7 p.m., so we left from home around one p.m. We left that early because we wanted to visit the Schönbrunn Palace, my favourite place of peace and rest. We walked about 30 kilometres that day, from our house to the autobahn. From the autobahn we spent another 40 minutes riding. The dangerous part was hitchhiking on the autobahn. We had to be extremely careful, because some of the cars pulled into the slow lane and we thought they would pick us up. But when someone would stop to give us a ride, we had to run another 500 metres because it took the high-speed cars that long to stop. When we walked by the slow lane, we had to be close to the outside edge of the autobahn, because the turbulence from the cars and, more especially, the big trucks, could blow us off our feet.

When we got into a car and the driver realized that we were not Austrian, they became fearful. Then we would explain that we were refugees from Romania and, when they heard about church, they relaxed. We could see it in their faces.

It took us about 4 hours, and we were in Vienna. Once in Vienna, I already knew the streets, especially the trams and subways.

Before we got to Rob's apartment, Nicu explained to me that Rob and Mary were graduates of a theological seminary in Baltimore, Maryland, USA. They had come to Austria to open the church. Rob originally was from Czechoslovakia (the new Czech Republic) and Mary was from China. They were wonderful. They truly loved God. I saw in their faces the trust and compassion for me of a brother and sister, that day when they came to Hohe Wand. They had the same face as Jean, and I knew they were honest with me.

We went to the pastor's apartment first. Both Rob and Mary greeted us warmly and invited us in. Nicu was my interpreter, because he spoke a little English. Over time, we became good friends. We all became lost in time as we told our personal histories to each other. When Nicu and Ella started to talk with them, I just sat on a couch and listened. I didn't understand all that they were saying, but I listened. Later on, we put our coats on and walked to church together. Their church was about 20 minutes from their apartment. When I looked at the sign, the name of the street was Strassgasse.

The church itself was located in a basement suite that had apartments above it. It was a simple church – a big room with a pulpit, new chairs and a piano, which was played during the services. Behind the pulpit was a wooden cross on the wall. The walls were white. The floor was covered with grey carpet. In the back was a combined nursery and cloakroom. There was a small kitchen, too. It contained a sink, electric stove, refrigerator and lots of cabinets that Rob had made. There was always coffee – the women from the church made sure of that. The suite was very neatly fixed up. The room was also used after services for informal meetings over coffee.

At 6:30 p.m. that evening, people started to come to church. I saw many different men and women from other countries. I was amazed – "Hello" came in many flavours. They walked inside and their faces were full of joy and big smiles. About 10 minutes before it started, there were over 20 people there. Small groups – Chinese, Koreans, Romanians, Polish, Austrians, Russians, Americans, Czechoslovakians, and more – got together to talk. There were many married people, but some were single.

I met my best friends there in church – Steve and his wife, Beata. They were wonderful people. Steve was about 25 and Beata was 20. I talked with them and learned that he was originally from Yugoslavia and Beata was from Poland. I could see in their faces that they truly loved the Lord and walked in His steps. Steve attended Bible seminary in Vienna, and he occasionally replaced Rob when he was gone, or busy with something else. Steve was a linguist at heart, and was fluent in all of the major European languages. He became one of my best friends and surest translators. Also I have met there Billy Alexandros which was Steve's blood brother. Billy, he truly was an inspiration for me. He always spoke the word of God in so much patience, just like Rob. I always took his advice because I knew Billy was a real Christian. Later on he got married with Gabi who was another wonderful Christian and a young beautiful lady. I have often been to their place which was in Traiskirchen camp. Always their door was opened for me. They remained in Vienna after my departure.

When the service started, the whole church became very quiet. Then the people sat down. After a few announcements, the new visitors were invited to stand and be recognized. I stood up, said my name, and sat back down. The other visitors did the same thing. (There were many pregnant women! Then I realized there were lots of fruitful and multiplying new Protestants in Rob's congregation.) Then, everyone stood for the singing of a hymn. As we sat down, Rob started the message by reading the text from the Bible. Then he preached the Word of God. When Rob preached, he used English, but there were regular church members who simulta- neously translated his sermon into German, Korean and, sometimes, Romanian. The foreigners could follow the sermon in their own language by listening through an earphone. Language was usually not a problem for anyone, and I had Romanian friends who could translate from English to German or Romanian, so the sermons helped me to learn German better and faster. If I wanted to talk with a brother or sister from China, I had to get Rob's wife, Mary, to help me understand. Most of us knew 3 or 4

European languages. Anyway, there was a regular public address system so that everyone else could clearly hear what Rob said in English.

After the service, everyone broke up into small groups and spoke in their native languages. Then I saw the people go to the kitchen to get coffee or a soft drink with cake or biscuits. Nicu, Ella and the other Romanians and I served ourselves as well. On my first visit I didn't talk much, because I didn't know many from the congregation, only very few of them. I kept quiet.

At the end, Nicu, Ella and I had planned to go to the train station. There was a train from Vienna to Viener Neustadt and, from there, we were going to walk back home – another 30 kilometres at night! Rob asked us how we were to get back home. After Nicu explained, Rob offered to drive us home. We were very happy!

Around 10:00 p.m., when everybody had left the church, Rob, Mary, Nicu, Ella and I got into Rob's car and drove back to Hohe Wand. Rob knew the road very well.

When we got home, around 11:20, Rob and Mary wanted to turn the car around and go back to Vienna. I felt really bad, and asked them if they would stay overnight. They accepted. I was so glad that I could do something for them. Since Jean had left to live in Vienna, we had plenty of extra space for Rob and Mary. We ate a snack and watched the distant lights from our balcony. The autobahn was red and white with car lights. In Viener Neustadt, the beautiful lights could be seen perfectly in the distance. The weather was still cold, but that night was clear and lit by a full moon. In a little while, I was tired. I went to another room to sleep.

I awakened early the next morning and told my landlord, Robert, that my preacher and his wife had brought us back from church last night and they had stayed overnight in my room. Robert said that was no problem. I went and told Frau Huver that my preacher and his wife were in my room and asked if she would fix breakfast for all of us. Of course, she did it immediately. The Huver family was very respectful of religion. All Austrians are the same in that regard.

After we had eaten, I told Rob and Mary that I had to go to work. They were surprised that I had found a job in such a short time in Hohe Wand. I told them that God worked in mysterious ways. We prayed together before we left the house. On the way to Vienna, Rob and Mary dropped me off at work. It was like a dream. I still can't believe what a wonderful Sunday I had. I fell in love with that church. I felt they were truly my brothers and sisters, all of them. The people knew I didn't speak German well, but they came and shook my hand and said "hello" with a sweet smile. They knew how to provoke me... and not be alone. I felt like God had answered one of my prayers. I stopped looking for another church, and enjoyed that congregation until I left Austria.

> "And let us consider one another to provoke unto
> love and to good works: Not forsaking the assembling
> of ourselves together, as the manner of some is; but
> exhorting one another: and so much the more, as ye see
> the day approaching."   Hebrews 10:24, 25

My life changed. I didn't feel the same – there was something inside of me that filled me with joy. When I arrived at work that Monday morning with a big smile, my boss noticed it. He quickly smiled back at me. I sat down and told my boss everything that had happened on Sunday in Vienna. When I mentioned the church, he was proud of me. My boss had seen me when I got out of Rob's car. He asked if the man was Romanian. I told him that Rob was American, and he was my pastor. My boss didn't expect the preacher to bring me home. It was something unusual to see this happen. Then I told him they had slept in my room last night. He gave me a long look, with tears in his eyes, and said that was good.

I was working hard every day and, after work, I went straight back home. My boss always gave me a ride. I took a shower, ate, and went right back to my room to read the Bible. I felt hungry and the more I read, the more I wanted. The Word of God became real to me and alive. I remembered lots of things Grandpa had told me before he died. Jean took his place for a while. Because of all his support, my boss and I became really close, and like we were part of some family.

> "When a man's ways please the Lord, he maketh
> even his enemies to be at peace with him."
>   Proverbs 16:7

Later, my boss took me to his own house in Viener Neustadt. He had some construction materials in his garage that we needed to pick up. This was the first time I had been to his home. He and his family lived in a 3-floor block. His block had 8 apartments in it, and he owned all of them. I learned that he was in the taxi business in Viener Neustadt. When I asked him how many cars he had, he said over 40 – Volvos and Mazdas. I saw the garage where all the taxis were serviced, and his mechanic who worked in the garage. I knew he had several employees. We didn't go inside the house, because we were in a hurry to go back to work. It was about a 25-minute drive each way between Hohe Wand and Viener Neustadt. I remembered when Robert told me about my boss being a millionaire, but I truly didn't care about that... but he looked like one.

Saturday came and I prepared my clothes for the next day to go back to Rob's church. I had been anticipating it all week. I had called Jean and told him about the church I had found. He was really happy to hear about it. Then he asked me if I was going to go back the next week. I told him I was on Sunday, the Lord willing. Since I was going to be in Vienna, he asked me if I would like to visit his church, too. I said, "I'll be more than happy." I could go to Jean's church on Sunday morning and to Rob's church in the evening. We agreed to the plan for Sunday.

At the time, I was working for my boss from Monday through to Friday. Saturday and Sunday, I was off. That was the deal. My boss was very busy on Saturday and Sunday with his business, and he didn't have time for me except in an emergency. On Friday, I asked my boss if he would take me to the train station the next day, because I wanted to go to Jean's church. When he heard about church, he agreed. I told him I would like to leave at 10 a.m. He gladly agreed, but I had to be ready. I just felt God all over me and I knew it was His will.

Saturday morning was a beautiful, sunny morning, and the warm weather had changed everything in Hohe Wand. In the surrounding mountains there were lots of tourists. They stayed in small motels, or camped and cooked outdoors. I was ready on Saturday at 9:30 a.m., waiting for my boss with a small bag of food that Frau Huver had given to me just in case. (I always thank God for her concern for me.) At about 10 o'clock, I saw my boss's Volvo taxi coming toward my home. What joy and excitement! The tourists must have thought I was rich, because I had called the taxi up there to the mountains. They didn't know he was my boss. He stopped the car beside me and said, "I see you are ready to go."

He turned around immediately and we were on the road to Viener-Neustadt. My boss drove fast out of the city and we got to the train station in no time. I got down and thanked him. He even handed me some extra money and said, "Be careful in Vienna, and call me when you get back." I took the train (this time I had a ticket and got to ride inside) and travelled to Vienna. I watched the fields and houses, and cars on the autobahn. I sat quietly and relaxed until I got to Vienna.

When I got to Vienna, I looked everywhere for Jean. Finally, I saw him at the end of the terminal, looking for me. When I saw him, my heart leapt for joy. We shook hands and hugged like brothers. We left the station and sat down in a nearby park to catch up on each other's lives. I listened to him. His excitement and enthusiasm were infectious.

He had been living with Peter's family at their apartment. Jean told them all about me, especially our escape from Romania. They were excited for me to come and meet with all of them. Peter's family had lived in Vienna for more than 15 years and, therefore, language was no problem for him and the rest of the family. They had 3 small children, and the family was very active in church. They supported the church and enjoyed a good reputation. I told Jean about my new church. I described Rob and Mary and others from the church. We both got excited and we thanked God.

After our prayer, we walked to the subway toward Peter's family. Jean told me, "John, they're waiting for us." We travelled 6 stations, got out and then walked a few streets to Peter's home. It was an old neighbourhood, with old apartments and lots of small shops all around. I received a very warm welcome. We became friends in no time, especially since everybody spoke Romanian. From the beginning, Peter's family thanked me for helping Jean escape. Peter told me that their church was praying for someone to take the pastor's place when he was not there. I understood immediately how important my friend Jean was to them.

We walked into a small hallway, through Jean's room, and then into a large living-room. After that, Peter showed me the children's room. From there, we walked into another good-sized room where he and his wife slept. The last small room was both the kitchen and the bathroom – it had their tub in it. The walls were covered with Austrian traditional festivities and pictures of family. The furniture wasn't expensive, but it was in very good condition and was placed in perfect spots. The hardwood floors were covered with rugs and, in the living room, there was a large, colourful, ornate oriental rug. A big chandelier (a Romanian tradition) was placed in each room. The apartment was on the second floor. It had a large picture-window, which provided a great view of the street. Over coffee, we all sat around and swapped stories about our former lives in Romania. Peter told me when and how he left the country. He and his wife were from Moldova, a very poor region of Romania. We talked on over dinner and finally all collapsed, exhausted. Jean went to his room and I slept in the living room.

We woke up early the next morning and prepared for church. We left at about 8 o'clock and took the subway. We arrived after travelling through 4 stations. Their Romanian Baptist church was located in another church basement on Molargasse. When we walked down the stairs into the basement, I saw a big space, full of chairs. I met many, many brothers and sisters. All were Romanians so, of course, I got to talk our language freely. Truly, a wonderful group I met in there. But I noticed something very interesting: the pastor was American! He preached in English and sister Ana, a Romanian, was the interpreter, and she was placed on the right of the pulpit. This pastor did not speak Romanian – he spoke only English. Sometimes, when the pastor didn't show up, Jean took his place and preached the Word of God. It was hard for me to communicate with the American pastor, because I didn't speak English. I had to take someone with me to translate. For that reason, I didn't approach him socially. Everyone there got to meet me, and they all gave me a warm welcome.

I also got to talk with my sister, Ana. Later on, I met her family. Ana's husband was a man who feared God, and I was able to talk with him.

Anyhow, I wasn't much interested in being a part of that church, but I do respect and love all the brothers and sisters I met there. After a while, we went back to Peter's apartment. Peter's wife cooked for all of us a very traditional Romanian meal. I truly felt they had a special love for me. A great peace was in that apartment. The harmony was indescribable. We all enjoyed being together. Lots of prayers were lifted up on my behalf and for my strength for the future. Peter talked to me like I was his brother, and he had a lot of love for me. Our hearts became one and we trusted in each other.

After we had eaten, Jean and I went to the Schönbrunn Palace and walked around for a little while. We talked about all the wonderful new things God had helped us experience in Austria. I was happy, because my darkness was transformed into light. I didn't want to talk about the bad things from the past any more. I met Rob at home and told him my friend, Jean, would be with me that night in church, our church. Rob was very glad. He didn't know about our relationship pre-dating our arrival in Austria.

At around 6:30 p.m. we went into the church, talking with our brothers and sisters. We were happy to be here. Steve was with us and he was our interpreter. Rob and Mary met Jean, and they became friends in no time. It seemed as if we had known each other for years, but it was only my second week in that church. Some of Jean's other Romanian friends from his church where there, too. We all enjoyed being together.

After the service, I went back to Hohe Wand. Rob and Mary offered me a ride. I declined that time, because my boss would be waiting for me at the train station in Viener Neustadt. All I needed was a telephone to call him. Mary offered the church's phone. Before I called my boss, I called Peter's family and thanked them for their hospitality. Peter offered me a place to sleep any time I came to Vienna. When I was at his house, I got some telephone numbers so I could keep in contact with their church. They were willing to give all kinds of support, especially spiritually. Peter and I remained friends until I left Austria. I can never forget the care he showed me. Before I left Vienna, I called my boss and told him I was on my way back. Then I told Jean I had to leave and go home to Hohe Wand. He felt bad because I had to leave, but he understood. He promised me that, when he got a job and found his own place to live, he would let me know. It felt good to know he cared about me.

I left Vienna and, when I got to Viener Neustadt, my boss was in front of the train station waiting for me. He was like a father to me. He took me to Hohe Wand in no time, and immediately turned the car and went back. I knew he was busy and I didn't talk much. I also knew that my boss was always ready to serve others.

On Sunday of the third week, Nicu, Ella and I were back on the road to the church in Vienna. It was a beautiful, sunny day. We left Hohe Wand around 10 a.m. and walked to the autobahn to hitchhike. In about 30 minutes, 500 cars must have passed us. Finally, someone stopped and picked us up. We thanked the driver and tried to explain in broken German that we were on our way to church in Vienna. Once he understood, our benefactor relaxed. Then we all fell silent, in peace. That day, we had plenty of time to go and visit the Schönbrunn Palace first, to relax for a while. That was one of my rituals. In the afternoon, Nicu called Rob and told him that we were in Vienna, so Rob invited us to his apartment and, from there, to accompany him to church. We took another late afternoon walking tour of downtown Vienna.

Rob lived in a 3-floor walk-up. His apartment had a small hall. On the left was a very small bathroom, on the right was a kitchen with a very small shower in it and, in front, were two bedrooms. It was spartan – it had only a few rugs on the beautiful hardwood floors, and inexpensive furniture – but he and his wife added the elegance to that simple place. When I stepped inside, I felt joy and the presence of God. It was a perfect peace. I saw that external luxuries didn't interest Rob and Mary; their world was spiritual – the Lord's work. Simplicity and elegance through Christ – that was Rob and Mary!

Nicu, Ella, Rob, Mary and I went to church together. After church, Rob and Mary took us home. Sometimes Rob would stay with us when he took us home. At other times, he would return to Vienna that same night.

Nicu and Ella continued to attend Rob's church for a while, but eventually they stopped. They asked me to make excuses for them to Rob and the congregation. Several times I did, but I had to stop telling those little white lies. Eventually, I told Rob I couldn't answer his questions and changed the subject immediately. Nicu and Ella came very rarely, so I let them answer for themselves.

I went every Sunday, even if I had to walk all the way to Vienna. I didn't give up because of transportation problems. I talked with Rob about my occasional long walks, and he understood. Also, I told my boss the situation I faced every Sunday when I had to go to church, and he understood. He began dropping me off on Sundays at the train station in Viener Neustadt, and from there I took the train. Also, Rob's wife, Mary, and another missionary named Mary, would come to pick me up. At other times, other people from my church came and got me. Everyone helped me, so I had no more problems with transportation. Sometimes, I actually missed the exercise of walking.

The church became like a big family to me. I was always excited to go there. There I met many foreign missionaries. It was an "international congregation" from all over the world, but we truly enjoyed being together.

On many occasions, I ate at Rob's apartment. His wife, Mary, cooked. I never got full when she cooked (Chinese food, you know). I was from the countryside of rural Romania by way of city ghettos, so I had never heard of "oriental food" or "Chinese food". I learned about it from sister Mary, who was originally from China. She was a very good cook. Sometimes, when Rob or both Marys came to pick me up, they let me know, and I prepared some food for them. My favourite was baked chicken in garlic with potatoes, and garden salad with different dressings. I learned lots of new foods to cook and many new spices and different black sauces. Wok stir-fries were a favourite, especially with chicken – not those skinny Romanian chickens. BBQ wings were another favourite of mine, and they were good. Mary made the best rice I had ever eaten. She had special pots from China. I remember her parents sent it to her. Chinese food was very different from German or Italian food. It was certainly different from the Romanian food to which I was accustomed. Chinese food was very popular so, in Vienna, there were lots of Chinese restaurants. Rob and Mary helped me in so many ways: they came many, many times to Hohe Wand to pick me up and drive me to Vienna.

Sometimes they would come to visit and give me Bible tutoring. Rob was the one who impacted on my life the most, with the work of God.

> "And he gave some, apostles; and some prophets; and
> some, evangelists; and some, pastors and teachers;For
> the perfecting of the saints, for the work of the ministry,
> for the edifying of the body of Christ:Till we all
> come in the unity of the faith, and of the knowledge
> of the Son of God, unto a perfect man, unto the
> measure of the stature of the fulness of Christ:That

we henceforth be no more children, tossed to and
fro, and carried about with every wind of doctrine,
by the sleight of men, and cunning craftiness, whereby
they lie in wait to deceive;But speaking the
truth in love, may grow up into him in all things,
which is the head, even Christ."   Eph. 4:11-15

Rob loved to help people, and he had important teaching skills. He also frequently fed me and gave me a place to sleep when I had no convenient way back to my home from Vienna. We had wonderful fellowship together, and I always loved to be with him. Sometimes we walked through the forest in Hohe Wand, or in the streets of Vienna, talking about Jesus. I never saw him angry or worried. I never heard a word of curse or discouragement cross his lips. He was always ready to answer my questions, with so much patience and kindness. He didn't speak German well, but it was enough to guide me through the Bible. I saw his walk with God, and there was no doubt in my heart that he was devoted to Christ. He and his wife were a wonderful couple, and everyone loved them. They were simple, and yet you could talk with them about anything. They were happy with what they had. My new brothers and sisters came around me full of love, and that was because of Rob and Mary and their actions towards everyone in that church. Rob had a big influence over me, especially when he revealed Christ more clearly to me. I spent many nights in Rob's apartment, especially when my boss didn't come to work on a Monday. I would leave on Friday afternoon and come back on Monday evening. I just walked around the streets of Vienna and, of course, I ate my favourite food – chicken with German rye bread.

When I came back to Hohe Wand, I went to my room after dinner and didn't come out until the next day, when I had to leave for work. I stopped hanging around with other Hohe Wand Romanians. I had grown tired of their negative attitudes and incessant complaining. When they saw that I had separated myself from them, they reciprocated. The day when they found out I went to church, they laughed at me. I was a joke to them. But I took my religion very seriously, because I found out through the Bible that it was about eternal life and death. And I wanted to live, not die. I worked hard during the week and, at the weekend, I went to church to be with my brothers and sisters.

During this time, I developed another close friend – Steve, my interpreter. We talked deeply together about my religious feelings. He spoke Romanian very well. He took Jean's place in many ways. He knew I was lonely and he was the one to comfort me. He was there like a brother for me, especially when I needed one. We walked many times on the streets of Vienna, just to talk about Jesus and get lost in the crowds. He was a very devoted man and his wife was the same way. He gave me attention, especially in church, because I did not talk much unless someone prodded me to talk. I spent many, many nights with him.

Steve and Beata lived in Vienna, in a small apartment. They had two rooms and a kitchen. In the kitchen was a small shower. The bathroom was communal. They didn't have much furniture, just the necessities. They lived very simply, like Rob and Mary. Steve was in seminary and Beata worked. They didn't have children. Neither of them had family in Austria. Steve's parents were in Yugoslavia, and Beata's were in Poland. They had been in Vienna for 6 or 7 years. They were my best friends until I left Austria, just like Rob and Mary and the missionary named Mary. When we walked together, I was with my brothers and sisters. I loved them more than my relatives from my own country.

Now I knew there was a heaven... I was free, and not under a communist regime. I forgot all the bad things.

Cutting Old Romanian Ties

IT WAS SUMMERTIME. I WORKED HARD full-time for my boss, and I sent many, many packages to the Constantinescu family through Magdalena. I was doing everything possible to help them survive.

That summer, Magdalena stopped writing to me. The letters didn't come as they should and I did not know why. I remember some of her early letters mentioned that her church members were unhappy that my packages were coming through Magdalena. In their eyes, I was a "bad boy" or trouble-maker, and they were too holy... I never understood it. When I stayed with the Constantinescus at the farm, some of the members of the church would come to talk with me, pretending to try to help me; but now I realized they were just concerned that, because of me, the authorities might harass them.

There was nothing personally between Magdalena and me, other than just being friends in Christ. I had nothing but respect for Magdalena and her parents, especially for their help. She was the one who brought me the Bible at the hospital when I was in a critical condition. And her parents took me under their wing when I had no place to go. I knew they hadn't forgotten me.

But everything just stopped, so I suspected church pressure and government harassment. The last news I had was that Magdalena was working at a state bakery. I knew she did not make enough money to support herself and the family. Also, in her last letter, she mentioned something about the state authorities asking her questions about me. This is a Romanian pressure technique that I understood well, because I had been on the receiving end before. I had told Magdalena that there would be political obstacles, from both church and state, to my helping them. I explained to her that communists like to stick their noses into everyone's business, but I encouraged her to not give up. We would behave legally so they could not be abusive to her.

Another letter came – the last one – and I found out that the state did try to stop the family from receiving my packages. I knew from the beginning that all my letters were monitored by the communist government. The government wanted to break down the relationship between the Constantinescu family and me. I felt bad, because I had helped them so little in such a short time. My mind was concentrated on this family. I could not forget them. When I was a stranger, they came and took me in; I was naked, and they clothed me. I was sick, and they visited me. I didn't know what to do. I started to pray and pray about the situation, expecting some quick solution. It started to bother me.

Even my boss at work saw that I was worried. He asked me about it. I explained the problem about the packages being stopped by the government. My boss understood immediately, because he already knew about Romania and the communist regime. We both felt bad about the situation. During that time my boss took Jean's place, because I shared my heart with him. I was free to tell him everything. He was a man who understood my pain and situation, but also, I knew there was nothing he could do about it. I never understood why Romania was as it was to its people... so cruel. I knew very well that the Constantinescu family desperately needed my support. I found out later that it was the church that was balking over the packages. I wondered what influence the church had over the sending of the packages to the Constantinescu family. I thought we were all supposed to help each other, not hinder. I was truly confused. Later on, I learned that Magdalena was engaged to be married. That made me happy for her. I knew Magdalena would help her parents. That was the last news I ever heard about the Constantinescu family, but I trust in the Lord to meet them in heaven with my Lord Jesus Christ. I had to let everything go and think about the future. I called Jean and told him the situation.

Jean found a Pentecostal Romanian church in Vienna. Immediately we planned to visit it. The next Sunday, Jean showed me where it was, and then he left to go to his personal church. The Pentecostal Romanian church was full that morning. The preacher spoke Romanian and I could understand perfectly. I truly felt in love with that church, but the Romanian brothers and sisters weren't too friendly. That shocked me and, for that reason, I didn't get too close to them. One day after a service, I remained to see what kind of activities they had. Well, after the majority of the congregation had left, there remained a couple of small groups who apparently knew each other. They called themselves by name. An older man from that church saw me alone and he came and asked if I was new there. I said, "Yes, this is the third time I have come here, and nobody has talked to me yet." Then the man tried to excuse the congregation's unfriendliness by telling me that there were too many visitors to keep track of. I explained that I had loitered to seek contact and conversation, but I was still ignored. After 3 visits I still didn't know the pastor's name. He became defensive. I just got up from the chair, said goodbye and left. It was heart-breaking to see these things, especially from people of my own country. I wasn't interested in that church any more. From that time, I stopped visiting other churches because I didn't want to be neglected again.

> "He was in the world, and the world was made
> by him, and the world knew him not.
> He came unto his own, and his own received
> him not." (John 1:10-11)

I called Jean and told him what had happened. Then I walked to my favourite places for a while, until I had to go to my church. I called Rob in the afternoon and told him I was in Vienna. I didn't mention anything to him about the Romanian church, because it was so depressing. When I got to church, at about 6:30 p.m., the room was almost full. I sat in the place where I usually sat. My friends Steve, Rob and Mary, and others, saluted me with a warm welcome. Then Jean came a few minutes later, as did the other Romanians. After the service, we all talked together then, later on, everyone scattered to their homes. I remained and, of course, Rob and Mary gave me a ride back home. On our way home, we got talking about the service and how God was moving His presence over the congregation. The number of people in the church was growing very fast.

It was beautiful weather that summer, and I worked for my boss 5 days a week. One day, my boss took me to his home. Most of the time he drove the Volvo, which was his favourite. At his home, I met his wife for the first time. She and I had talked on the phone before, but we had never met each other. When we got inside the house, she greeted me very kindly. I looked to her just like my mum. Also, a young boy, who was probably 17, sat in his room and didn't speak to me. I could feel the spirit of prejudice – he was not happy that I was there. We never talked to each other for the entire time I worked for my boss.

The three of us walked into the kitchen and we sat down. My boss's wife served us home-made food. It was excellent, especially since I was hungry. After an hour, my boss and I went to his garage. I met his co-worker, who was working on one of his Volvos. His name was Frank. He was understanding and friendly with me. I stayed for a while, and then my boss took me back to Hohe Wand. My boss's wife had told me to tell her if I needed anything and she would help me. She was a very wonderful woman with lots of compassion for me. I had told her I loved Jesus Christ and I attended a church in Vienna. I don't know if they were saved, but they sure showed me love and help through their actions. It was as though we had known each other for a long time. I became a part of their family. Money was no longer a problem, nor were the bad memories from Romania. Poor Romanian immigrants were often treated like second-class people in relatively rich Austria. However, I experienced none of that with my boss and his wife. I knew God was with me and I didn't have to worry any more.

"And we know that all things work together
for good to them that love God, to them who
are the called according to his purpose."
(Romans 8:28)

I always thanked Him because of all the blessings He gave me. I told my boss many times that God had put us together for a reason. He never said much; he just nodded in agreement. I worked hard for them and they loved me and respected my Lord, work and loyalty. They also fed me well, because they knew that Romanians were always hungry. My favourite food was vegetable soup with pork in it, and heavy rye bread. My boss's wife was a wonderful cook and she enjoyed stuffing me when I ate with them.

Now everyone at Hohe Wand knew me. Whenever I went, I was recognized and greeted by people I'd met in the camp. Being a stranger in that small mountain town didn't last long. Soon, no car passed without offering me a ride. The locals picked me up, no matter where I was walking. We may not have known each other's names, but we knew each other's faces and hearts.

One day I went to work and learned from my boss that a civil war had started in Romania. I was shocked. I called Jean, who had already heard the news the preceding night. We surmised that the communist regime had brought the country so low that the working classes had rebelled, and the army was powerless to stop it. The people had seen and suffered enough. The beautiful garden that Romania used to be had been turned into a living hell by President Nicolae Ceausescu and his wife. Millions of Romanians had become "refugees" in their own land, internally displaced people whose sole desire, like mine, was to escape to freedom, to the West.

The Ceausescu Family
Bites the Bullet

It was September 1989 when President Nicolae Ceausescu and his wife left to visit the countries in Asia Minor. That is when the people rebelled and the bloody civil war ensued. The president returned immediately, but the generals of the Romanian army were waiting for him. He was speedily and summarily tried by a military tribunal, and condemned. Then he and his wife were taken straight outside and shot dead. It was on 25 December 1989. The news spread all over Europe; the executions had been filmed and there was talk of nothing else.

Most Austrians were glad that the Romanian communists were out of power. I had lots of friends who walked out of Austria and returned to Romania. The new regime changed the laws so that everyone could return home. Romania assured refugees that no criminal charges would be pressed for leaving Romania. The new government was also willing to help pay for our return. I thought about it, but there was nothing to make me return. Yes, I had all the memories and negative feelings inside of me but, with my mother dead and my wife gone, I had nothing to lose. So, I kept walking forward and not looking back.

> "No man, having put his hand to the plough,
> and looking back, is fit for the kingdom of
> God."   Luke 9:62

I wanted to see more of the world, especially since I had invested in new languages. I was ready to be positive and to have a future which I had made. I also thought that the communists might regain strength and take over again. Then it would be worse than before. I just could not accept that. Friends wanted me to return with them, but I refused. At that time, my trust was in God and I knew that one day He would take me from Austria to a promised land. I was in another world, and I had another new family there, namely the church and my boss, who cared for me and loved me. I could not give that up. There were people around me whom I had never had before, full of love and kindness, so I turned away from Romania and let the Lord move me. About a week later, my boss asked me if I would go back. I said, "No, boss, and I have never thought about it." He was happy with my decision. Then he told me that Romania was destroyed to the ground and would need a long time to come back up. I agreed with him, because it was true. When the subject of the Romanian revolution came up, I made sure everyone knew that I was not going back. I had a new home, and new family and friends. I couldn't endure the heartache of a return to Romania.

In September I needed new clothing, because the weather changed. One day my boss brought me back home, as he normally did. He backed the car up to my front steps and stopped, then opened the electric boot. I wondered what he was doing. There were two big plastic bags inside. My boss told me to take them out – I still didn't know what they were. As I took the bags out and set them on the steps, I felt the clothes inside. Then he told me that his wife had told him to give me the bags. I closed the boot and he took off, telling me to be ready at 9 o'clock tomorrow for work. He disappeared in no time.

I took the bags to my room to see what they contained. I was all alone in the room. I closed the door behind me and opened the bags. I was speechless – they were full of clothes and shoes. I couldn't believe it. I cried that night. I saw two nice suits, one brown and the other navy blue. Both of them fitted me perfectly. Shirts and T-shirts, underwear, socks, blue jeans, a few pairs of shoes, and lots of big towels! I thanked God with all my heart. He will seek after me. Long ago I would not have understood, after this experience, I immediately understood what he had meant. It took me an hour to relax. Nobody knew how I felt inside, only God. Most of the clothes still had the labels and prices on them. I was shocked at how much my boss's wife had spent on me. Now I wouldn't look like a homeless ragamuffin any more. I would look like an Austrian, not a poor immigrant.

Robert came up to my room before dinner and saw my new clothes. He understood my delight. I decided to call my boss's wife at home and thank her. I had the telephone number in my Bible. I went downstairs and asked Robert if I could call my boss at home. Robert knew the number and he called it for me. When my boss's wife was on the phone, he immediately handed the telephone to me. I thanked her in German. She understood what I meant. I still remember all these things.

Later on, the weather got worse. October was cold, wet and windy. It was foggy almost every day. It might clear up for a few hours but, most of the time, Hohe Wand was in the clouds. My boss was still taking care of me, even if I didn't work. Most of the time I stayed home in my room and read the Bible. I was taking it easy, because I knew there was nothing I could do. I took a vacation for a few months.

I started to visit Jean in Vienna. We spent more time together. During that time, Jean was working for an engineer as a watchman. He had his own separate room, which was very large, and I spent weekends with him. He was happy there and, most of the time, he was busy with his church. I went to Jean every week and I stayed at his place for two or three days. I walked all around Vienna, sight-seeing. I always went to my favourite places, where I truly enjoyed the relaxation. I visited brothers and sisters, Romanian or Austrian. We spent a little time together and, after that, I would walk on. I would visit my church and return to Hohe Wand. Of course, my boss took me home.

I stopped travelling to Vienna in November because of the heavy snow and icy roads. Instead, I hung around with my Romanian Christian friends and with Herr Huver's family. I established a schedule. Every day, I took a walk through the snow, enjoying and feeling myself free. Most of the time I walked alone; that way, I could talk to God and myself.

Another Austrian Christmas

TIME WAS GOING BY QUICKLY AND everything was going smoothly. Before I realized it, the Christmas season was upon us. I remember the beautiful German hymns and carols. At Christmas, everything about Vienna changed! All the businesses and streets were festively decorated. The Viennese wore festive holiday costumes. The normally curt and business-like Viennese became relaxed, open and friendly. The place and the people were beautiful. Everyone had packages in their hands, wrapped up in beautifully coloured paper. It was like another world. People prepared themselves for these holidays. Everyone was bustling; the city was in perpetual motion. Markets overflowed with people haggling over prices. I saw more real Christmas trees than I knew existed. People wore big smiles. I understood the liberty they had. It was an exciting time. By now I knew what Christmas meant. I had a new perspective. Oh, what excitement in listening to my pastor, Rob, talking about God coming down in the flesh as a little baby! He spoke with so much enthusiasm in the church. We all enjoyed his sermons. It reminded me of when my grandpa told me about the "little baby Jesus," and especially his purpose for coming into this world.

> "For the Son of man is come to seek and
> to save that which was lost."   (Luke 19:10)

I just wanted to thank Him for the wonderful changes in my life. What excited me most was the way all of free Europe celebrated Christmas. I saw many cars coming from other countries to the mountains of Hohe Wand. In the place where I lived, Christmas was a big movement, too. The cold snow and icy roads didn't stop the tourists, especially from Vienna. Polyglot Europe descended on the mountains to vacation and play.

My church family invited Jean and me to a Christmas celebration. There was no question, because I was a part of the family. I remember that I called Jean and asked him if he would come and be a part of my family. He accepted. Oh, I was thrilled, because we could celebrate once again together and, of course, in the church family.

The time came and I was on my way to Vienna. I prepared a big plate with potatoes, salad and a big fried chicken. That was my favourite food. I bought 3 big German cakes from a store. They were delicious, especially the one with chocolate on top. My sister, Mary, came and took me to Vienna. Before I left, I had told my boss that I was going to church and I would be spending the night there. He was so happy when I told him, because he knew I would be in a safe place.

I went directly to the church and set out my food with everyone else. I was pleased to be able to contribute food and join in the giving. Everyone had been helping me, so it was my chance to give something back, even if it was largely symbolic. It was about 4 o'clock in the afternoon when we arrived. I took a walk to Kartplatz. It was cold and snowy, but beautiful, too. The snow on the streets melted quickly but, in the parks, it stayed. I sat and enjoyed the beauty around me. Then I went to a café for hot coffee. I had a blue denim jacket, thick black trousers and black leather boots on. I was very comfortable, because they were very expensive. I looked like a young Austrian, not a poor immigrant. I bought a big coffee and sat for a while, looking out the window.

Then I went to visit Peter's family and greet them for Christmas. They were all busy because they were expecting some Romanian families that evening for the celebration: all the members from the Baptist Romanian church. Peter promised me that he would bring their Romanians to my church and they would stay for a while. I called Jean and asked him what time he would be arriving. He promised me that he would be there for the start of the programme.

After that, I walked to Rob's house to help. He and his wife had a lot of food to carry, and gifts to take to the church. There were 8 of us carrying everything. A few other members had arrived before us. We shook off the snow and cold, and welcomed each other. We planned to celebrate for the whole night. I wasn't concerned with how I'd get back home.

By 6:30 that evening there were over 80 people at church, and they were still arriving. There weren't enough chairs; the little church was packed. The entire congregation showed up that night. I got to meet some parents and extended family members whom I had never seen or met before. At about 7 p.m., the service started and pastor Rob preached the story of Jesus Christ. I was very excited and thrilled to be there. We were all family. My friend Jean came, too. Many Romanians from Peter's church visited. Nicu and Ella came back, too. After the service, everyone remained to share fellowship, food and gifts. Steve, my interpreter, and his wife were there, too.

The main topic of conversation was how our lives as refugees were changing and improving. Our futures were as bright to us as the Christmas lights all around us. We were from different parts of this world. We were learning new trades, new languages, new cultures and new self-esteem. Each one of us was expecting to fly somewhere new and strange in the New Year. Though we all made many plans, they didn't always come through. But we had every reason to maintain our optimism – so many people were helping us and loving us. Starting over was no longer a burden, but was an adventure. We were so thankful for Austria accepting us and helping us to reach our final destinations. We said lots of prayers in Austria.

It was different now for me, because my thinking had changed. From the beginning, we asked each other about our chosen new countries. I had originally selected Australia but, when that changed, I did not become discouraged, because I knew I had to go somewhere. Wherever I was to go, I knew Jesus would be there, too. Rob and Mary remained in Austria as gatekeepers and facilitators for the dreams of many immigrants. There were many young men and women refugees who were my age, who talked with me.

I came to realize that Jesus Christ was among us. I knew He heard all of our conversations and He was pleased because we all included Him in our plans. Our trust was in Him and we trusted that He could move us. We knew that Jesus had a plan for every one of us to accomplish His purpose.

Our festival table was full of different kinds of German food, cakes, and bread for sandwiches. This was an alcohol-free night, too, but we had soft drinks, most of which were new to me. I tried them all. When I reflected on all I had been through, I realized that all the pain and suffering I'd experienced had been worth it. I had a new life, and I was a "new creature in Christ, old things are passed away; behold, all things become new." I was so happy that I had someone to listen to me and to share my heart at church. Jean and I talked for a long time and, after recounting all our adventures, we laughed. I truly felt we belonged to each other.

Later that night, I spoke to Rob. I opened my heart and made an oath before him. I told him that I wanted to be baptized, but not in some kind of tub. He understood, and I was glad that he agreed to baptize me. Then I requested that it be in some river. He said, we will do it all in May, when the weather warms up." We decided on the River Danube. I had experienced a lot of personal danger with that river, but now it would be a part of my salvation in Christ. After that, Rob told me that I wasn't the only one to make such a request. I couldn't swim, but I trusted my Lord Jesus. He wouldn't let me drown. I was very excited about the prospect of a spring baptism. I thanked Rob. I was looking forward to the spring.

At about 3:00 a.m., some of the brothers with their wives told us that they had to leave, because of their little babies at home. At about 4 o'clock in the morning, the celebration ended. I won't forget the excitement and friendship; especially talking to Lord Jesus. We were all of one mind and one accord and one purpose for our lives. There were many prayers and commitments made that night. I stayed there and slept in the church with other brothers. The floor carpet was just perfect for me, especially with the warm air blowing from the electric heater. There was lots of food left over; I had no problem with that.

I stayed another day in Vienna, at Rob's apartment. After that I was ready to leave for home. Rob took me back to my home at the Huvers' house. I asked him and Mary to stay with me for a couple of days. I knew they needed a little break from the church. They stayed overnight and, the next day, they went back to Vienna.

When I got back to Hohe Wand, I called my boss and told him that I was home. He was happy. First, I talked with my boss's wife, because she answered the telephone. She asked me if I needed anything. I said, "No, I am all right, thank you." He had stopped working at the new house until after the holidays. This was in 1989-1990. When all the holidays were ended, I went back to work with my boss. He suspected that I'd return to Romania, and asked me again if I wanted to go back. I said, "No, I will not return." Romania was firmly in my past. I continued to go to church in Vienna every Saturday afternoon. On Monday morning, I would return to work.

My First Car

In February 1990, Rob called me and told me that he was going to buy another car and that he was giving the old one to me – a dream come true! I was so excited that I couldn't sleep for two nights. I had to go to Vienna to pick up the car. It was my first. It was a white Fiat, with 4 doors, blue seats, carpet on the floor, electric windows, and a leather cover on the steering wheel. It had 5 speeds and 4 cylinders. When Rob handed me the keys to the car, I acted like it was nothing. But, inside, I was ecstatic. Many times, I had thought how much I would like to have such a car – how careful I would be with it, and what good care I would take of it! It was an unarticulated desire, but God knew it all. I realized He wanted me to stop worrying about myself and put more focus on Him, not in the things of the world.

"But seek ye first the kingdom of God, and his righteousness;
and all these things shall be added unto you.   (Matthew 6:33)

I thanked Rob and God for the blessing. Rob told me that I needed to buy some tyres and check the oil. I took the car and drove straight to Hohe Wand. On my way, I stopped and showed my boss the car. He told me that it was a piece of junk. Well, it might be for a wealthy man like him, but to me it was luxury and the best car ever. I drove to Hohe Wand and all my friends saw my car. They were happy for me, but some of them were jealous. I told everyone that this gift came from God because I obeyed His commandments. Some of them laughed at me, but I didn't care. The Huver family was happy for me and they said that if I needed any help to tell them.

The roads were very difficult in Hohe Wand because of thick ice and the snow. I had to be very careful when I drove on those roads, especially since the car had rear-wheel drive and I hadn't bought new tyres. I drove all around Hohe Wand and to Viener Neustadt.

Around a week or so later, I was returning from my boss's home. It was the middle of February and the road in Hohe Wand was really icy. About 300 metres from my house, there was a very dangerous curve. I did not pay attention and I forgot to slow down. Eventually, I found myself flying through the air, and I knew something was wrong. When it was over, I had slid off the road and rolled the car on to its side. Two tyres supported the car, and the other two were suspended in the air. I really didn't know what had happened. I gathered my wits and wiggled my fingers and toes, and then I got out. Lack of experience and icy Austrian roads don't mix. I tried to push the car back down on all four tyres, but I couldn't.

I went to my nearby friend, an old Austrian man, and explained what had happened. He laughed at me. Together, we pushed the car down and it fell back to its normal position. He then gave me a quick driving course on how to handle icy roads. He told me that I was lucky to learn my lesson so cheaply. I took his instruction seriously, because I knew that any future accident that I might have on a mountain road might not end so well. I could lose my life on any big curve from Hohe Wand.

After he had finished, I thanked him for his help and lesson. He knew that I had no prior experience of driving on ice. In Romania, I had never driven a car. No one I knew had one. I certainly couldn't afford a car. After giving me instructions, he told me to get in the car and crank it up. When I started the car, the radio was turned up loud. I was embarrassed for him to hear it. He told me that the radio was a dangerous distraction in bad weather. Again, my friend was right and I nodded in agreement. After a few more pointers, I drove him to his home.

When I examined the car, I discovered that the body wasn't bent or scratched. I was amazed. I knew it was indeed a cheap lesson. That evening, I thanked my Lord Jesus for saving me from my own ignorance. I repented immediately, because I came to the realization that the car was not for me. I was being too wild. From that night on I trusted God to take care of my car and me. I took driving seriously, especially on the autobahn. I was driving at 180-200 kilometres per hour, but now I drove no more than 120 kilometres per hour. (At that time the speed limit on autobahns was non-existent.) I never had another problem with that car.

It ran very well. My car didn't measure up to Austrian standards, but it was all that I had. I was truly happy with it.

When Rob decided to give me the car, I said in my heart that I would help anybody who needed it. It was a promise to God. When I thought back to the past, and thought about how much had been done for me, I couldn't say no to anyone who requested my help. When I remembered how God blessed me with the car, I felt obligated to help others. I was not counted just to travel and see the beauty of Austria for myself.

I helped lots of my friends and their families from the camp in Transkirchen. They had many children and, on Sunday morning, they wanted to take them to the Pentecostal Romanian church, the one in Vienna where I had been ignored. It pleased me to give back. I told them that, when they needed a ride, they should call me and I would be there in no time. I told them that they would not have any more problems with transportation. Whenever I went to Vienna, the car was packed with between 8 and 10 people. We put towels over the windows so nobody could see how packed the car was. I went with them to church, listened to the message and brought them back.

I felt I was doing the will of God. I gave many, many rides to Nicu and Ella, to the grocery store and elsewhere. At the time, two Romanian friends were living with me in Hohe Wand. They were Francesco and Allen, and neither of them was Christian. Francesco was about 50 and Allen was maybe 27. We were pretty close, and we helped each other in many ways. Francesco kept me abreast of all the gossip in Hohe Wand. We had a lot in common, and I was closer to them because they were single like me. I took them, many times, wherever they needed to go. All it cost me was money for petrol, but I wasn't worried, because my boss paid me well.

Moving to Vienna – the Centre of the Civilized World

SPRINGTIME CAME ONCE AGAIN, and the weather changed. The trees took on their normal, lush green colours and the flowers punctuated the season change. The thick snow and ice melted, and the water flowed quickly down to the valley. It was beautiful. I started working with my boss again, and we were happy for another year. I was very happy because, by that time, I could speak fluent German. I could carry on a conversation with anybody.

In April of 1990, my friend, Jean, asked me if I wanted to move to Vienna. I agreed immediately, but I didn't know how to find a place to live. He said to ask at Transkirchen, because they had all of the information. Of course, I told the camp authorities that I would pay the moving expenses from my own pocket. They immediately gave me an address in Vienna, and I went to look for the apartment.

After two hours, I finally found the street and the building with the apartments. I walked to the third floor and went to the manager's apartment. She was young and was originally from Russia. She was about my age and she owned the whole building, which served the immigration department. She was expecting me, because she had received a phone call from the immigration people. We introduced ourselves, and I told her that Transkirchen had recommended her to me. She checked my identification papers, and I had a room in about 20 minutes. I was really tired and I lay down on my bed and fell asleep immediately.

When I woke up, I called Jean to tell him that I had a place. However, my boss wasn't happy, because he thought that I would give up on him; but I continued working for him.

I woke up at about 7:30 a.m. and, at about 8:30, I was in the train station at Viener Neustadt. My boss picked me up because the train station was on his way, and we went to work together. After work, he dropped me back at the train station and I went back to Vienna. I bought a Euro pass for the whole month, because it was cheap. My boss paid for it – thank you, Lord! I let my church family know, and they were happy for me. I just felt that God was moving me and supplying my needs. I was really close to the church. Sometimes I would park my car at my boss's house and walk, just for the exercise. I parked my car at my boss's home. I realized that the car was nice, but it was also a financial drain.

Now that I was in Vienna, the car was an unnecessary expense. I decided that I would be better off without my little Fiat. I asked my boss how I could sell the car. He made a few calls around, but nobody wanted to buy it, although it had served me well.

Where I lived now there were more people who were Russian, Polish and single, like me. They were also immigrants waiting to go to the USA. I had one room with a single bed and a small table at the side. It had a hardwood floor and was located on the third floor. I shared a refrigerator with others. It was a public kitchen with three gas stoves. The bathroom with the shower was also communal. At night, the gated entrance to the building was closed at 10 p.m.

To America

A⊤ ᴛʜᴇ ᴇɴᴅ ᴏꜰ Aᴘʀɪʟ, I got a call from immigration. I had to present myself immediately at the refugees' offices. When I got to Transkirchen, Jean was waiting for me. He told me that Australia had denied my entry. Very calmly I said, "That's all?" He was expecting me to get angry and to say unpleasant things. I wasn't worried any more, or angry, because I knew that God wanted me in another place. Then the men from our office told both Jean and me that we had to present ourselves to the US Embassy and, the same day, we went there and a man asked me if I wanted to go to America. I said, "I don't mind."

I didn't think about myself any more, and thanked God for sending me there. I counted on Him because I belonged to Him. I was a born-again Christian and I feared nothing. I knew the Lord was with me and that He had a better plan than I did, so I didn't resist God. This time I obeyed Him. I truly was ready to see more of this world. I knew God was in control, and my worrying would change nothing.

My friend Jean was accepted by Canada, because the Baptist church sponsored him. We rejoiced at his good fortune. After that, we walked outside the building and went to a little porch to sit on a bench. My mind was darting from thought to image to thought. America, America – the most blessed country in the whole world! Who had not heard about America? That country was much-respected. Fear came through my body. Yes, the riches of the world were in that country. No country could compare with America.

We sat on the bench, lost in thought and silence. After a while, Jean asked me if I was pleased with America. I had no immediate answer for him, but I said, "I don't know much about it, but I know one thing – it will be better than Romania. And the further away, the better it will be." I told him there was nothing to worry about. God had prepared everything for me. As long as I seek Him, He will never abandon me or forsake me. I told him that I knew one thing – Jesus loved me and that's all that mattered. I knew no English! But I knew that I was able to learn new languages – I had just done it with German. I knew God would take care of all that. He would teach me another language in America. I was also learning Italian, which was very close to my native Romanian.

I called Rob and asked if I could talk with him, and then I went to his apartment. He and Mary were waiting for the news. I explained that the USA had approved my immigration and that Australia had turned me down. I explained that I was going to America – anywhere but Romania. When I told him, he wasn't too happy to hear it. No excitement or smile was on his face, like there usually was. It was a long moment until he said, "So you accept the USA?" I said that I had no other choice. Both of them looked into my eyes, but I'd stopped the conversation. Then Rob asked me if I knew where in America I would be located. I said I had no idea, but they would let me know before I left Austria. There was silence. I knew something was wrong, because Rob had never acted like that before. Rob knew me very well, so I knew he was worried.

After a while, I asked him if the USA was a good destination. He said that it was. Then he continued and said, "You may have to start over and find yourself a good church and job." But that was my whole purpose in going to America: to start a new family. I didn't want to be a millionaire, or rich, because I knew riches would turn my heart from the Lord, but I was looking for a better life and job, and a chance to serve God. That was in my heart. Then Mary said, "John, you'll be all right; just don't get into trouble, like drugs or wild living." After that, I went to my place in Vienna.

On the second morning, I went to Viener Neustadt, to my boss, and told him everything that had occurred the day before. He and his wife were very excited. They were happy for me. He was concerned about me because Australia had denied me asylum, but now I could go somewhere to be free. After that, we went to work together in Hohe Wand and I went to see the Huver family. I told them that the USA had accepted me and I would fly soon to America. They were happy to hear the good news.

On the next Sunday, I went to Jean's church and announced my choice to the church. They were all happy for me. That day, Peter invited me to his apartment to celebrate. Another family came and I felt the love of them all towards me. There was exceptional joy in our hearts. I remained with Peter's family until 6 o'clock that night, and then I left for my church. When I got there, I told Rob to make the announcement to the church. Of course, he did, and everybody was happy to hear it. After the service, my friend Steve came and hugged and encouraged me. He sat down, and we talked for a while.

I also visited Francesco, who was my Italian teacher, and Alan, as well as Nicu and Ella. Alan had taken to the Austrian farming life. Francesco was still unemployed. He spent most of his time at the Huvers' house. Francesco told me that he had been to Italy 5 or 6 years ago and knew Italy very well. I told him that visiting Italy had always been a dream for me, since before I had left Romania. I already had a tattoo, on my left shoulder, of a palm tree, and I was looking forward to actually seeing one. He was happy to hear that. In fact, Francesco and Alan were all set to emigrate to Italy. It was their destination of choice, but Italy was closed to immigration. The refugee camp there was full, but Francesco had a few relatives in Italy and they were waiting for the papers from the government to be approved. So, by his staying at Hohe Wand, he was able to give me lots of pointers on how to travel in Italy. His advice proved most useful. He helped me make all my travel plans. We planned my Italian holiday for the spring.

An Italian Holiday

It was beautiful weather in May 1990, when I visited Italy. I travelled illegally, but it was only a minor peccadillo. I went to the train station in Vienna at night and I took the "International", which came from Hungary through Austria and terminated in Rome. I travelled all night. When the conductor came to check papers, I went to the bathroom and locked the door. I knew that he was going to knock and I answered with a very gentle "yes?" I also knew that he would walk away, because he trusted me to have a ticket. In the morning, at about 6 o'clock, I arrived at the Austrian-Italian border.

The train remained in Austria and all the passengers had to walk to the new train on the Italian side of the Brenner Pass. The sight was beautiful. A high alpine forest surrounded the Brenner Pass. I didn't stop or gawk, because the Italian police patrol could tell that I was a stranger. Since I didn't have proper travel papers, I wanted to blend in with the Italian travellers and walk across the border to re-board the train to Bologna. When I walked close to the train, the Italian conductor looked at me and I acted like I was really tired. I didn't pay any attention to him. I walked around him. Then I got on the train and feigned fatigue. I lay my head on the bench and the conductors left me alone. They probably knew I was an undocumented traveller, but they didn't want to be bothered. Francesco had coached me. I trusted him because he encouraged me so much to visit places where he had been. There was really no legal penalty other than a return ride to Austria and an official scolding. By then, I spoke fluent Italian with no accent. When the conductors vanished and we were under way, I got to look at the fields and forests. The train was "supplementary", which connected the "International" between the Brenner Pass and Bologna. In Bologna was the real "International", which continued and ended in Rome.

When I got to Bologna, the train station was not very big. There were 3 cashiers for the train tickets, some food machines with soft drinks, a cigarette machine, and a small waiting-room for the travellers. I never saw so many friendly people. They greeted me and I greeted them back and smiled. I talked with a few of them and they realized that I was not Italian, but they truly didn't care. As a matter of fact, they told me to be watchful of the policemen for the streets, and I was. The city of Bologna looked pretty big. I felt like I was in another world, because everything had changed around me. Outside the city, between the border and Bologna, were mountains and lots of private houses and property around. I saw hundreds of kilometres of vineyards and orchards: apples, pears and peaches. I thought that I was in a new heaven – the vegetation was much lusher than in Austria. Also, there were small businesses everywhere you looked. The most popular brand of car in Italy was Fiat. Most of the cars in Italy are very small, and only the wealthy drive big cars because petrol in very expensive.

I took a train to Rome. The travel time between Bologna and Rome was about 3 hours on the "International". I was glued to the window to see the sights in between: cities, small towns, bridges, mountains and, of course, lots of water – especially in the south. Finally, I got to Rome, but I didn't spend much time there because my desire was to go to Naples, not Rome. I wanted to see the palm trees there. I had to hang around for another hour until the train to Naples arrived. The Rome train station was a hub of railway tracks that went in all directions. It was a very old building made of huge rocks. After an hour, the train to Naples arrived at the terminal. I changed trains to Naples – another two-hour leg of the trip. The train to Naples was full of very loud, boisterous passengers... not like polite Austrians. But I didn't mind – it made me feel welcome. At least they were friendly. The terrain changed radically between Rome and Naples. I just sat calmly, but with so much enthusiasm inside me about my visit. I was excited to be a carefree traveller. Nobody recognized where I came from... maybe it was better they did not know. There was a big difference between Austria and Naples.

When I arrived in Naples, I saw the big train station. Hundreds of people were moving about. It was a tall, spacious, new building made of glass but, upon closer inspection, I was put off by the nastiness and lack of maintenance. I left the train station and walked around the centre of the city, which was also unkempt. Downtown Naples was dirty and littered. Trash was everywhere: bottles, papers, clothes, and even furniture on the corners of the streets. The streets were smaller than I had anticipated. The people gawked at you and they sounded very strange. Laundry was strung overhead all over the place. It wasn't what I expected. Naples was worlds away from the towns of northern Italy. Even the dialect was different – it was the dialect of Sicily. I wasn't pleased.

I walked out of the downtown area and things began to look much better. I finally saw the palm trees that I had wanted to see for a long time. They were beautiful. That was the first time I'd ever seen them. I will never forget that time.

At 9 o'clock in the morning it was 90°F. The weather was beautiful. You didn't need much clothing in that heat. I decided to walk to the Mediterranean Sea, which could be seen and heard from the city. When I got there, I walked along the shore. I felt like I was walking on pillows! It was hot. Then I stopped for a while and I looked all around – nothing, just an infinity of water. I left for a while and went back to the city to eat. I stayed there on top of big rocks. The shore was a little bit farther from the city. I heard the furious water breaking on the big rocks, not the noise of the city. I stayed and watched the sun set. It was beautiful. There were so many colours; it was like a rainbow reflected from the water. I felt so little.

"Thou hast beset me behind and before,
and laid thine hand upon me.
Such knowledge is too wonderful for me;
It is high, I cannot attain unto it.
Whither shall I go from thy spirit?
Or whither shall I flee from thy presence?
(Psalm 139: 5-7)

The sound of the water put me to sleep. I slept on the beach all through the night. I knew God was with me and protected me from all evil, because I was his child. I was worry-free. I woke to another beautiful view. I saw the blood-red sun reflecting off the water of the Bay of Naples. The reflected colours changed as the sun rose. The sea was like glass. I sat there almost all day, just to look and admire the wonderful works of God. I stayed in Naples for two days, but most of my time I spent on the seashore, among the palm trees.

After that, I returned to Rome, another place I had longed to see since my days in Romania. I had heard so much about this famous city. Now it was a reality for me. Oh, how good it is to be free! I took another passenger train back to Rome. As I left Naples, I said goodbye with tears in my eyes.

After two hours, I arrived in Rome. I picked up a free map of the city and began to walk around. I walked around the streets of Rome for two days. My eyes had never seen such old, strong buildings. The streets were laid 1500–1800 years ago, from red brick. They were very narrow and didn't have much space, just enough for one car. I was deeply impressed by Rome. The ancient buildings were ornate and imposing. I was transported back in time.

I saw the Coliseum and walked inside its arena. It was a fearful place of human sacrifice and death. That arena spoke to me: I heard their voices; I can still hear them. I was out of place and out of time – just a stranger. When I reflected on the things that must have happened there in ancient times, it made me sad. The old walls stared back at me angrily – those still standing strong. I was in the place where Christians were slaughtered for their faith and fed to the hungry lions. I felt so unworthy to serve Christ when I thought of those who had suffered for His kingdom. I didn't have to suffer, because Jesus Christ suffered for me on the cross. He took all of my suffering and pain. All I had to do was rely on the Creator. I sat there for several hours, just thinking. After that, I walked back to the streets.

The streets of old Rome were full of small markets and small businesses. I got to see so many different kinds of fish and seafood that I had never seen before. Italian cities were always in motion, day and night. Cars and people everywhere were constantly moving. At night, Rome was another live city, full of beauty. I stayed in Rome for two days, and then I went to Venice. That was another train ride that lasted several hours.

It took about 3 hours to get to Venice. I had to travel back north to get there. On the train with me were many, many tourists going that way, ready to go with their cameras in hand. That afternoon, I finally got to Venice. I realized that I was approaching because of all the water around the train. When I got down from the train, I saw a huge train station. It was bigger than the one in Naples, but there was another big difference. In Venice, even the train station was quiet. The people were well-mannered, like Austrians, not like those rowdy Neapolitans. There was a restrained cacophony of different languages. I got a map of the city and studied it. Venice wasn't as big as I had thought. The beauty of the buildings was dazzling. All the tourists were as excited as I was, especially by the churches. Most of the ancient buildings were surrounded by water. The world-famous Venetian glass was well-displayed in the churches. I was also amazed to see so much water. Not many streets, but many canals. There were boats everywhere: speedboats, gondolas, even tour boats. I saw St Maria, a place you can reach only by boat. Venice was much more than I had heard about in Romania and Austria. The old, huge blocks were set in perfect designs.

The markets were full of fresh vegetables, seafood and, of course, famous Italian cheese. I ate the best bread, pasta and rice. You can always smell the freshness of bread and you could see that professional bakers had made the bread – it was snow-white and shaped into long loaves, a tradition of Italy. Oh, the spaghetti with Parmesan cheese – I could never get full. The lasagne, with tomato paste and cheese mixed all together was stupendous! It was a luxury for me. I didn't see much meat, but I did have Italian sausage and salamis.

Like Naples, the Venetian dialect took some time getting used to. Venice was different from Naples. These Italians were very elegant and wore expensive clothes. Italians are like Austrians; they love coffee with different kinds of sweet cakes. Truly "La Dolce Vita", which means "sweet life." People also loved red wine. I walked everywhere and truly enjoyed myself. On both nights, I heard traditional Italian music and enjoyed the parties. Beautiful songs on the water could be heard from the professional singers on the long, black boats called "gondolas". I'm glad I have seen Venice before I die. I will never forget it.

After two days, I travelled back to Bologna. Before I left Venice, I shed another few tears of joy... it was so picturesque, so romantic. Then I changed trains at Bologna for Vienna. When I got back to Austria, I thanked God for letting me see it all. It had taken me the whole week to visit the 3 big Italian cites. We always walked alone, Jesus and I. I have a great amount of respect for the country of Italy.

Industrial Strength Baptism

WHEN I RETURNED TO AUSTRIA, it was beautiful weather. I no longer needed to wear a jacket. It was the last week of May. I went to my friend, Rob, to see how things were going. He said he had missed me in Vienna. I told him about my visit, and he was shocked that I had ventured off alone. But this was one of my dreams that had come true.

Rob told me that he had a long list of baptismal candidates. We planned our Danube Baptism for the middle of a week. The weather was still beautiful. I called Jean to see if he wanted to come and to be part of it. He accepted. Also, he told the other Romanians about the Baptism. Thirty of us got together to take the subway from the church to the Danube. Rob and others had already selected a spot on the riverbank. We travelled to the Danube station and then we walked about 30 minutes to the river. It was a perfect location. It was a 1000-metre walk to a beautiful stretch of white river sand, with bushes and grass at either end. We took food and drinks with us, and a couple of balls to play with. When we got there, the weather changed and the sky was full with clouds. But we did not give up.

We had a little meeting and prepared to get wet with Jesus. We all had on white gowns. Eight of us were to be baptized. We attracted lots of spectators. When Rob began to read the Bible and explain to us the meaning and the purpose of baptism, something very interesting occurred that I had never seen before. The sky became dark with clouds but, in that spot, we were enveloped in sunlight. I felt like the Lord was shining over us with His presence. I bet we looked special to the spectators, and to God! We sure felt blessed.

I felt Jesus and the peace that passed all understanding. I washed away all of my bad habits that day. I knew I was still a soul in progress, but I was beginning to turn away from my old life. I had lots of habits that had remained from Romania. I knew exactly what it meant for me to be baptized. Yes, I was following the example of Jesus, which is what I wanted to do. I fixed my heart on Him and not the others around me. This was a business for life and death, it was not just temporary – I took the action very seriously and I let nothing distract me.

Before I got in the water I felt the cold wind, which had just started to blow. I was the seventh one to be baptized. I walked to the water and, as I stepped in, it felt like ice water. I kept going towards Rob. Finally, I got between Rob and Steve and I heard Rob saying a prayer for me. Steve was my interpreter, and he told me every word Rob spoke. I confessed to God, all my sins. After that, I laid on my back in the water. I was submerged, and then both brothers helped me to get up. I walked out and changed my clothes.

Oh! I will never forget that day. I was accepted into God's family, and my name was written in the book of life. I wasn't perfect in my heart, but that was no excuse to wait. I realized that, without Jesus, there was nothing. I kept going to church and reading my Bible, but now I was more committed to it.

After that, I went to my boss and told him I had been baptized in the River Danube. My boss and his wife were excited and were proud of me. I always thank God for them, because they did wonderful things for me. I kept my job and stayed with my boss. When he didn't have to work because he was too busy, I found a replacement with part-time work. But I never left my boss. I knew of his concern for me. Many times, he called me to his home and his wife fed me well. They wanted to make sure that I got what I needed. They had no other children, just one son, and he didn't care about his parents. I was upset about that, but there was nothing I could do.

I finally got a telephone call from Jean. He had to leave Austria to go to Toronto, Canada. I felt something would be missing from my heart. When he told me the news, I was speechless for a few moments. I knew my friend was truly free, just as he desired. I went to Peter's house, because I wanted to go to the airport to see Jean off to Canada. When I got to Peter's apartment, it was full of people from his church. When they saw me, they said, "John, we are going to miss your friend!" Tears came to my eyes, and I hugged Jean. He promised me he would write to me – and he did. It was the beginning of June; the weather was beautiful and hot. I knew in my heart that soon it would be my turn to leave Austria. I told my boss on the phone that Jean had gone to Canada. He was delighted for him.

I knew that I, too, had to start over and learn a new culture, traditions and, of course, another language. I spoke no English, not a word. I knew I had to face new obstacles and new language barriers, but that no longer bothered me. I was confident; I no longer dwelt on Romania. I had adapted to Austria in a very short time, because life there was good. I also knew I was going somewhere even better. As a matter of fact, I even stopped trying to call or write to Romania because I knew these efforts were dangerous for the people I tried to contact. It might sound selfish, but letting go was actually in the best interests of those I still loved. I didn't expect much from life – just to be free.

After Jean left, I spent most of my time around my boss, at his home or at work in Hohe Wand. The weather was beautiful and hot. I enjoyed Vienna, except when I had to work. I still walked to my favourite park, the Schönbrunn Palace. I took some sandwiches with me so that I could stay longer. In the evening, I went around to Saint Stephen's Cathedral and to Kartplatz. There, Rob preached in the street almost every week about Jesus Christ. Oh, what wonderful moments, especially when crowds stopped and Rob caught their attention. Afterwards, when he had finished preaching, lots of people came to him with different questions in different languages. I met no Romanians at Rob's street-preaching episodes, but there were lots of Austrians, Poles, Czechs, Chinese and others. I prayed for them to receive the gospel and God's plan for salvation.

Preparing to Jump the Pond

AT THE END OF JUNE, I received a letter from immigration instructing me to present myself to the US Embassy in July. I knew that my time was up, and I told my church family about having to go to the US Embassy. They were all pleased for me.

Then I called my boss and told him the good news, but he said to come to his home to talk. The next morning, I went to his house. When I looked at my boss's face and his wife's face, I knew something was wrong. After we had eaten, he told me, "John, I know in a short time you will be leaving for America." He told me that, if I didn't like it, I should call them and they would send me the money to return to Austria. I was speechless. They were very sad that I was leaving, but I was ready for a new beginning, not looking back any more. When I left, my boss handed me money in dollars, and I asked him what it was for. He said it would help me. I thanked him and, after that, I left.

When I went to the US Embassy, they asked me if I was ready to leave on 24th July to fly to America. I said that I was and, sure enough, I signed the papers. Before I left, I was instructed about what I could take and what I could not. I really didn't take much because I knew that, when I got there, the Lord Jesus would provide for me. God had always been faithful to me. I knew He would not give up on me now. I was excited and happy to see another land of milk and honey. I knew I would not be alone there. Though I didn't have relatives or friends, Jesus was with me. I came to realize that money had no value. I knew in my heart that God brought me out from the communist country. He provided for my needs in Austria, and I knew He would do it again. I was completely worry-free. I had been in the same situation when I arrived in Austria. I knew the USA would be no problem for me. I knew inside that I was as free as a bird mentally, spiritually and physically.

Everybody knew that I was flying to America. I relaxed and stopped working. Most of the time, I was with my brothers and sisters in Christ. I wanted to spend the last days around them.

On 24th July, 1990, I said goodbye to everyone, including all my friends from Hohe Wand. I found myself at the airport with a small suitcase, which contained a few clothes, and a few dollars in my pocket. A representative of immigration was there, waiting for me. I told him my full name and he handed me my ticket. He showed me the terminal where I had to go. I boarded the plane and sat down in my seat. It was my first time on a commercial aeroplane, but I wasn't afraid, because I knew who was in charge. I thought to myself that my time in Austria was over.

I thanked and praised God for all the blessings He had given me daily in Austria, and especially for the people He had brought into my life. I had so many good memories and so much respect for the Austrian people. I knew that, if I didn't see them again, I would see everyone in heaven with Jesus.

The plane wasn't big. We flew to Munich, Germany, first. After one hour, I boarded a big Swissair plane. That was the plane that brought me to the USA.

> "And we know that all things work together for
> good to them that love God, to them who are
> called according to his purpose."   (Romans 8:28)

Proverbs 3:5-6 (K.J.V.)

Trust in the LORD with all thine heart; and lean not unto thine own understanding.

In all thy ways acknowledge him, and he shall direct thy paths.

Romans 10:9-10 (K.J.V.)

That if thou shalt confess with thy mouth the Lord Jesus, and shalt believe in thine heart that God hath raised him from the dead, thou shalt be saved.

For with the heart man believeth unto righteousness; and with the mouth confession is made unto salvation.

Hebrews 10:24-25 (K.J. V.)

And let us consider one another to provoke unto love and unto good works:

Not forsaking the assembling of ourselves together, as the manner of some is; but exhorting one another: and so much the more, as ye see the day approaching.

Proverbs 16:7 (K.J.V.)

When a man's ways please the LORD, he maketh even his enemies to be at peace with him.

Ephesians 4:11-15 (K.J.V.)

And he gave some apostles; and some prophets; and some, evangelists; and some pastors and teacher;

For the perfecting of the saints, for the work of the ministry, for the edifying of the body of Christ:

Till we all come in the unity of the faith, and of the knowledge of the Son of God, unto a perfect man, unto the measure of the fullness of Christ:

That we henceforth be no more children, tossed to and fro, and carried about with wind of doctrine, by the sleight of men, and cunning craftiness, whereby they lie in wait to deceive;

But speaking the truth in love, may grow up into him in all things, which is the head, even Christ;

John 1:10-11 (K.J.V.)

He was in the world, and the world was made by him, and the world knew him not.
He came unto his own and his own received him not.

Romans 8:28 (K.J.V.)

And we know that all things work together for good to them that love God, to them who are the called according to his purpose.

Luke 9:62 (K.J.V.)

And Jesus said unto him, No man having put his hand to the plough, and looking back, is fit for the kingdom of God.

Luke 19:10 (K.J.V.)

For the son of man is come to seek and save that which was lost.

Matthew 6:33 (K.J.V.)

But seek ye first the kingdom of God, and his righteousness; and all these things shall be added unto you.

Psalm 139:5-7 (K.J.V.)

Thou hast beset me behind and before, and laid thine hand upon me.
Such knowledge is too wonderful for me; it is high, I cannot attain unto it.
Whither shall I go from thy spirit? Or whither shall I flee from thy presence?

Romans 8:28 (K.J.V.)

And we know that all things work together for good to them that love God to them who are the called according to his purpose.